Learn Computer Vision Using OpenCV

With Deep Learning CNNs and RNNs

Sunila Gollapudi

Foreword by V Laxmikanth

Apress®

Learn Computer Vision Using OpenCV: With Deep Learning CNNs and RNNs

Sunila Gollapudi
Hyderabad, Telangana, India

ISBN-13 (pbk): 978-1-4842-4260-5   ISBN-13 (electronic): 978-1-4842-4261-2
https://doi.org/10.1007/978-1-4842-4261-2

Copyright © 2019 by Sunila Gollapudi

Managing Director, Apress Media LLC: Welmoed Spahr
Acquisitions Editor: Celestin Suresh John
Development Editor: Matthew Moodie
Coordinating Editor: Shrikant Vishwakarma

Cover designed by eStudioCalamar

Cover image designed by Freepik (www.freepik.com)

Distributed to the book trade worldwide by Springer Science+Business Media New York, 233 Spring Street, 6th Floor, New York, NY 10013. Phone 1-800-SPRINGER, fax (201) 348-4505, e-mail orders-ny@springer-sbm.com, or visit www.springeronline.com. Apress Media, LLC is a California LLC and the sole member (owner) is Springer Science + Business Media Finance Inc (SSBM Finance Inc). SSBM Finance Inc is a **Delaware** corporation.

For information on translations, please e-mail rights@apress.com, or visit www.apress.com/rights-permissions.

Apress titles may be purchased in bulk for academic, corporate, or promotional use. eBook versions and licenses are also available for most titles. For more information, reference our Print and eBook Bulk Sales web page at www.apress.com/bulk-sales.

Any source code or other supplementary material referenced by the author in this book is available to readers on GitHub via the book's product page, located at www.apress.com/978-1-4842-4260-5. For more detailed information, please visit www.apress.com/source-code.

Printed on acid-free paper

To my angel, my BFF, my raison d'être—my daughter, Sai Srividya Nikita—for being proud of me always!

Table of Contents

About the Author

 **Sunila Gollapudi** is an executive vice president at Broadridge Financial Solutions India (Pvt) Ltd. Sunila is a passionate and pragmatic technology leader with more than 17 years of experience in architecting, designing, and developing client-centric, enterprise-scale, and data-driven solutions. She oversees every stage of the technology implementation and is a thought leader and technology visionary with a proven ability to build the technology road map. Primarily focused on the banking and financial services domain over the past ten years, she is a data connoisseur and an architect, adept at designing an overall data strategy to maximize the value of data through analytics. She is also an author and a mentor with an entrepreneur mind-set who believes in continuous learning as a key to organizational growth.

Her specialties include building overall intelligent automation strategies by synthesizing the business and domain drivers and emerging technology trends in Big Data engineering and analytics; leading cloud migration and DevOps strategies for CI/CD; and steering application (legacy) modernization, reuse, and technology standardization initiatives.

About the Technical Reviewer

 **Lentin Joseph** is an author and robotics entrepreneur from India. He runs a robotics software company called Qbotics Labs in India. He has more than eight years of experience in the robotics domain, primarily in ROS, OpenCV, and PCL.

He has authored several books on ROS, namely, *Learning Robotics Using Python*, *Mastering ROS for Robotics Programming*, *ROS Robotics Projects*, *ROS Programming*, and *Robot Operating System for Absolute Beginners*. He is also the technical reviewer of six robotics books.

He completed his master's in robotics and automation in India and also conducted research work at the Robotics Institute, Carnegie Mellon University, in the United States.

Acknowledgments

My sincere thanks to Broadridge for providing an opportunity to champion the adoption of artificial intelligence in the financial services domain. Special thanks to my mentor and boss, V. Laxmikanth, the managing director at Broadridge India, for all the support and trust and for taking the time to pen the foreword to this book. I always value and look up to your humility and leadership.

A big thank-you to Apress, the publishing team, and the reviewers for an opportunity to work with you and for being efficient, patient, and professional.

My heartfelt gratitude to Mrs. Radhika Laxmikanth for her unflinching support and to my brothers, Ravi and Sashi, and my close friends for giving the best encouragement and being the best critics.

Finally, kudos to all the technology enthusiasts who constantly experiment and inspire me to be a student for life!

Foreword

Building machines that can see and interpret things around us is an interesting, but notoriously complex problem to solve. The human visual system is infallible for tasks such as recognizing a face or a given object.

Computer vision has now become a very important sub-field of artificial intelligence. Application areas of computer vision have expanded from reading and interpreting human scripts (handwriting recognition) or analyzing images and videos to using these capabilities in security surveillance and intelligent automation (among other digital usages).

In this book, Sunila Gollapudi articulates the broader vision of artificial intelligence and how computer vision is now a key enabler. She has included a step-by-step hands-on guide to building computer vision applications from scratch using OpenCV and Python. Readers can access the complete code for each of these implementations, which utilize real-world examples and open data sets.

Overall, what is more challenging is how computer vision applications can be integrated as an offering to enhance existing products or applications, and how they can be scaled and deployed as a service. This book has a special focus on operationalizing AI applications and cloud platforms for computer vision.

—V Laxmikanth
Managing Director
Broadridge India
www.broadridge.com

Introduction

What artificial intelligence is today is a result of our continuous pursuit to make machines do all that humans can do, be it hearing, seeing, perceiving, thinking, or emoting. The evolution of artificial intelligence has reached an interesting juncture where machines not only are doing intensive work that is beyond a human's physical capabilities (such as mining harmful chemicals, large manufacturing plants, etc.) but also are being companions or assistants to humans by helping with day-to-day chores and by being available on small devices like smartphones (for example, Siri, Alexa, and Google Assistant). The key measure for success now is how personalized these machines can be and how well they can operate in collaboration with humans (human-aware AI). While this is reaping bigger benefits by enhancing quality of life and improving the adoption of technology in many businesses, it is also opening up avenues for misuse, probing the need for governing bodies to define stricter boundaries and controls around adopting artificial intelligence.

Computer vision is one such area of artificial intelligence that has significantly gained adoption in recent times given the advent of the Internet of Things. Computer vision is all about enabling machines to perceive and interpret what is seen.

This book focuses on the field of computer vision in particular and provides step-by-step guidance on how to build computer vision applications to address real-world use cases using OpenCV with Python. This book briefly introduces the overall landscape of artificial intelligence and its purpose and subfields, which includes computer vision. That is followed by a detailed introduction to computer vision and its subfields such as OCR, ICR, and OMR that enable computers to view, recognize, and process images and videos in the way human do and provide the necessary interpretations.

This book starts with setting up OpenCV with Python from scratch and then covers implementing specialized image processing, implementing object/feature detection and motion tracking functions, using advanced libraries, and productionizing large-scale deployments using OpenCV.

The high-level objectives of the book are as follows:

- Understand what computer vision is and its overall application in AI and intelligent automation systems

- Learn all the deep learning techniques required and used for building computer vision applications

- Learn how to build complex computer vision applications using the latest techniques in OpenCV using programming skills such as basic Python and NumPy

- See practical applications and implementations such as face detection and recognition (face swapping and filters!), handwriting recognition, object detection, tracking, and motion analysis

This book has seven chapters, described here:

Chapter 1, "Artificial Intelligence and Computer Vision," focuses on introducing you to the landscape of artificial intelligence and the role of computer vision in AI applications. This chapter explains what images are, describes their characteristics, and introduces some computer vision concepts such as manipulation, tracking, detection, and recognition. It also describes some use cases and domains that need this technology.

Chapter 2, "OpenCV with Python," introduces an open library called OpenCV that provides the tools and necessary frameworks to implement computer vision applications. A brief introduction to Python and the image libraries of Python like NumPy is provided. You will be able to set up an OpenCV/Python environment from scratch and get ready to implement some real-world use cases for the upcoming chapters. Additionally, the chapter talks about some aspects around computer vision as a service and discusses the extended libraries of OpenCV like OpenCV.JS for web and mobile applications and how OpenCV can be deployed on the cloud. A few competing frameworks and tools like the Google Vision API from Google, Textract and Rekognition from Amazon AWS, and the Microsoft Computer Vision API are introduced.

Chapter 3, "Deep Learning for Computer Vision," describes how building computer vision applications requires creating complex deep learning models with two components: a convolution neural network (CNN) that transforms an input image into a set of features, and a recurring neural network (RNN) that turns those features into a rich, descriptive language. This chapter covers how these cutting-edge deep learning architectures work, especially in the context of computer vision.

Chapter 4, "Image Manipulation and Segmentation," covers image manipulations and segmentation-related functions that are core to image processing in computer vision. For each of the use cases, the syntax and implementations of the built-in functions in OpenCV in Python are covered, and sample implementations are provided. Techniques such as edge detection, rotations, resizing, shape detection, and so on, are covered in depth.

Chapter 5, "Object Detection and Recognition," provides a deep dive into object detection and then moves on to object recognition followed by face-feature recognition, landmark identification, and finally handwriting recognition. The necessary OpenCV libraries are explained, and sample implementations are provided.

Chapter 6, "Motion Analysis and Tracking," covers motion analysis and tracking of objects in videos. Information about different types of objects in motion is given, with details on how to remove background and foreground information and how to do real-time tracking. The topics in this chapter are an extension to the object detection and recognition techniques in Chapter 5.

CHAPTER 1

Artificial Intelligence and Computer Vision

The field of artificial intelligence, and its application in day-to day life, has seen remarkable evolution in the past three to five years. Artificial intelligence (AI) is an enabler that potentially facilitates machines doing everything that humans can do. This includes perceiving, reasoning, rationalizing, and problem-solving while working within a context or interacting with the environment with more efficiency and accuracy. Here, the word *context* means the domain or the business where the problem is dealt with, for example online shopping, social media, insurance, manufacturing, and others. Interacting with the environment could mean that computers or machines work along with the humans or take input from external stimuli and adjust their behaviors accordingly. Computer vision, which enables computers and machines to see and understand the world around them, specifically has become a game-changer for how and where machines can be used and AI can be adopted.

This chapter covers the larger AI dream that is all about touching both the personal and professional lives of humans and how computer vision among other areas is a key enabler. Also, you'll learn about a few real-world applications, challenges, and technology tools such as OpenCV that help in complex implementations.

© Sunila Gollapudi 2019
S. Gollapudi, *Learn Computer Vision Using OpenCV*,
https://doi.org/10.1007/978-1-4842-4261-2_1

The following topics are covered in detail in this chapter:

- Artificial intelligence and its landscape, which includes a basic definition and the usage context of robotics, intelligent automation, natural language processing, expert systems, speech recognition, computer vision, and machine learning

- Computer vision, including its challenges and applications in today's world

- Computer vision architecture and tools, including what images are and how to understand and manipulate key attributes of images

- A sneak-peak into the core building blocks of computer vision and aspects such as image manipulation and segmentation, object detection, motion analysis and tracking, and others

- A brief introduction to optical character recognition, intelligent character recognition, and optimal mark recognition

---

Note   A good understanding of programming and prior knowledge of Python will be helpful to understand the working examples in this book; however, primers will be given for all the hands-on code exercises.

Introduction to Artificial Intelligence

The definition of *artificial intelligence* has evolved since its first reference in 1956 at a Dartmouth conference, from emulating how the human brain works to solving focused, complex problems to doing all that a human can do such as seeing, hearing, communicating, acting, learning, perceiving, thinking, deciding, demonstrating emotion and compassion, interacting with environment, and more. The 2012 AI breakthroughs with vision, language recognition, and self-driving vehicles changed the way that AI is looked at today. This section gives a simple and informal definition of artificial intelligence.

Essentially, AI is the field of computer science that involves enabling computers to behave like humans or perform tasks that usually require human intelligence.

The purpose of AI systems is evolving. In this section, we will cover different types of AI systems categorized based on their core purpose. You will also observe how these different types of AI systems signify a step toward building smarter systems.

Figure 1-1 lists different types of AI.

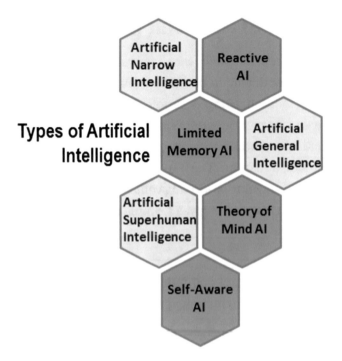

Figure 1-1. *Types of AI*

- **Reactive AI** was the first kind of AI that was talked about. These types of machines do not have memory and do not use information from past experiences. In these machines, the current context is directly perceived as it is and acted upon. This makes the machine behave the same way every time it encounters a situation. The benefit of this is a reliable and consistent outcome. An example is Deep Blue (a chess-playing computer developed by IBM that won against Kasparov in the game of chess).

- **Limited memory AI** machines look into the past and use it as a preprogrammed representation of the world and then apply it to the current data set. For example, in self-driving cars, decisions on when a car should change lanes is based on data such as lane markings, speed limits or road directions, current speed of the car, and relative neighboring car speeds.

- **Theory of mind AI** machines are intelligent machines that use advanced technologies that have more to do with understanding human emotions. The *theory of mind* is a psychological term that refers to the fact that living beings have emotions and thoughts that determine their behavior.

- **Self-aware AI** machines are an extension of theory of mind AI. They can configure representations, which means we will have machines that are conscious and aware given a context. This is also called *human-aware AI* or *human interaction AI*. There are no prototypes built of these machines.

Type of AI	Memory	Uses Past Experience	Interaction with Environment	Dynamic and Incremental Learning	Examples
Reactive AI	No	No	No	No	Deep Blue
Limited memory AI	Yes (with little information)	Yes (a limited set that become preprogrammed standards)	No	No	Self-driving cars
Theory of mind AI	Yes	Yes	No	Yes	Efforts in progress
Self-aware AI	Yes	Yes	Yes	Yes	Efforts in progress

Another way of categorizing of AI systems is based on the degree of complexity of the problem at hand.

Artificial narrow intelligence (ANI) is about solving a problem against a given request with a narrow range of abilities. A feature like Siri in smartphones can be considered an example in this case. This is also called *weak AI*.

Artificial general intelligence (AGI) is referred to as *strong AI* and refers to a machine that is as capable as humans. The Pillo robot is an example of a robot that can diagnose an illness and administer pills as well.

Artificial super intelligence (ASI) is about machines that can perform tasks beyond what humans are capable of. The Alpha 2 robot was a first attempt toward this; it is a robot that can manage a smart home and operate things at home. It potentially could be a member of the family. Most of the existing AI today is ANI. AGI and ASI are still being developed.

Figure 1-2 represents the core functions and features of an AI system at the center and related subfields that support implementing these functions.

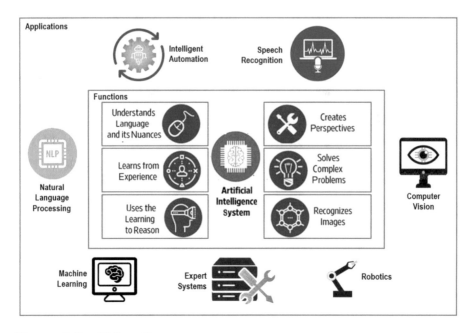

Figure 1-2. *AI functions*

The applications or subfields of AI are as follows:

- Natural language processing

- Robotics

- Machine learning and deep learning

- Expert systems

- Speech or voice recognition

- Intelligent automation

- Computer vision

Each of these subfields is interrelated, and any real-world implementation usually includes one or more subfields. The next sections define each of these subfields and give real-world examples and related technology tools wherever applicable, before taking a deep dive into computer vision.

Natural Language Processing

Natural language processing (NLP) refers to an area of specialization in computer science that deals with analyzing and deriving useful or meaningful information from natural language or human language. At a high level, this requires employing formal techniques such as tokenization, relationship extraction in the context of a specific business case, word classification, and sentence detection. For a language, *syntax* refers to basic rules the language follows, and *semantics* refers to its meaning. The complexity comes from the fact that the meaning of text can be ambiguous and can change with the context. For example, the word *saturation* could have different definitions when used with colors or when used in the context of human behaviors.

NLP is used in a wide variety of disciplines to solve a variety of problems. A brief list of applications follows:

- **Searching** refers to identifying specific elements of text within a bigger context of content.

- **Machine translation** is about translating text from one natural language to another and summarizing longer text in documents, blogs, and so on.

- **Named-entity recognition (NER)** refers to extracting the names of locations, people, and things from text.

- **Information grouping** is about categorizing text based on its content and context.

- **Sentiment analysis** is usually used to perceive and provide automated help or feedback on how a product such as a book or a movie is doing in the market.

- **Answering queries** or **help** is used in medicine or retail services, for example in chat bots.

- **Speech recognition** helps analyze and understand automatically the context in a conversation with humans.

Table 1-1 describes some key NLP techniques and provides examples.

Table 1-1. *NLP Techniques*

NLP Techniques	Description	Example
Sentence segmentation	This technique is all about breaking up the text and marking the sentences within the text, usually identified by dot (.) separation.	**Input:** We went to Naigara Falls. That was fun! **Output:** Sentence 1: We went to Naigara FallsSentence 2: That was fun!
Tokenization	This is a technique to identify the different words or punctuation marks or symbols given in a sentence.	**Input:** This movie has a funny story line but has a "tragic" end. **Output:** [This] [movie] [has] [a] [funny] [story] [line] [but] [has] [a] ["] [tragic] ["] [end][.]
Named entity recognition	This is a technique to identify different entities within a sentence such as a person, place, time, and so on.	**Input:** The Singapore Fintech conference starts at 9 a.m. **Output:** Time, location, event
Stemming/ lemmatization	This technique trims the words to extract the root word.	**Input:** Starting, Started, Start **Output:** Start

(*continued*)

Table 1-1. (*continued*)

NLP Techniques	Description	Example
Part-of-speech tagging	This is a technique to identify different parts of speech and tag them as noun, verb, adjective, preposition, pronoun, and so on.	**Input:** Since it was late, she stayed back. **Output:** BP: Verb noun third person singular present form IN: Prepositions and subordinating conjunctions PRP: Personal pronoun PRP: Personal pronoun
Parsing	The parsing technique is about walking through the sentence to mark different words in it.	**Input:** Sylvie and Andrew went to watch a movie. **Output:** (S(NP(NP Sylvie and (NP(Andrew)) (VP(went VBP to watch (NP a movie))))

Robotics

Robotics is a computer science discipline that deals with the design, programming, engineering, and development of physical robots or machines that are built to execute tasks that are usually done by humans.

The adoption of robotics was originally targeted for jobs that are hazardous for humans such as welding, riveting, mining, cleaning toxic wastes, or defusing bombs, among others, or those that need high precision or have low tolerance for human errors such as long surgeries in the medical field.

While robots have been around and evolving for several decades, it is only now that the use of robots in day-to-day activities is picking up. With the advent of the Internet of Things (IoT) and Big Data, the assimilation of a large number of streaming data points and analysis is not a challenge. For example, if you look at a simple sensor on an autonomous vehicle, it processes hundreds of thousands of data points every millisecond or second to assess whether a move by the vehicle is safe and aligned to reach the target destination within the stipulated time.

Machine Learning

Machine learning is a way of building intelligence into a machine so it will be able to learn over time and do better using its own experience. It deals with a pattern search mechanism that filters the relevant details from the details or environment.

Machine learning algorithms that are constructed in this way can build up intelligence. The goal of a learning algorithm is to produce a result in the form of a rule that is accurate to a maximum extent.

Figure 1-3 depicts various subfields of machine learning.

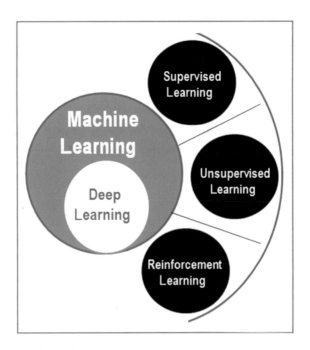

Figure 1-3. *Machine learning*

Supervised learning is working to a known expectation, which means that what needs to be analyzed from the data is defined up front. When there is no clear target in mind or specific problem to solve, the learning is referred to as *unsupervised learning*. The goal in this case is to decipher the structure in the data first and then to identify potential output attributes. As an example, to train a puppy, rewarding him every time he follows instructions works well. In fact, he figures out quickly what behavior helps him earn rewards. A learning methodology that focuses on maximizing the rewards from the result is referred to as *reinforcement learning*.

Deep learning is an area of machine learning that focuses on unifying machine learning with artificial intelligence. For a face detection requirement, a deep learning algorithm records or learns features such as the length of the nose, the distance between the eyes, the color of the eyeballs, and so on. This data is used to address a classification or a prediction problem and is evidently different from the traditional shallow learning algorithm. In Chapter 2, we will cover some specific deep learning methods that are used in computer vision.

Expert Systems

Expert systems (ESs) are one of the most significant research domains of AI that were first mentioned at Stanford University. These systems primarily focus on solving complex problems in a particular domain at a level of exemplary human intelligence or expertise. Expert systems are highly responsive, reliable, accurate, and performant. While they cannot replace a human when it comes to decision-making, they are used as advisors to humans and can help in diagnosis, explanation, prediction, justification, and reasoning. Any expert system includes three core components: a knowledge base, an inference engine, and a user interface.

Expert systems are used heavily in many domains. Some examples of usage are fraud detection (the identification of suspicious transactions and stock market trading in the financial domain), critical ailment diagnosis and deduction of root cause for an ailment in the medical domain, and prediction of the potential behavior of a system by monitoring its current status against the patterns derived from earlier monitoring reports.

Speech and Voice Recognition

Speech recognition technology enables computers to recognize spoken words, which are then converted to text for analysis. A natural progression in processing includes the application of NLP techniques on the extracted text. *Voice recognition* is a subset of speech recognition with one of the goals of identifying a person based on the voice. Today, many electronic products such as mobile phones, TVs, and electronic gadgets support speech recognition to enable smart and automatic operations based on simple instructions. There are advanced services such as Siri, Alexa, and

Google Assistant from technology giants such as Apple, Google, and Amazon, among others, that are breaking barriers in simplifying day-to-day activities.

Intelligent Process Automation

Automation has evolved from running repetitive and mundane tasks to dealing with complex cases and optimizing overall the way humans execute tasks. *Robotic process automation* (RPA) is the application of technology that allows a user to configure a software robot (*bot*) to capture and interpret existing applications for processing a transaction, manipulating data, triggering responses, communicating with other digital systems in an efficient way, and scaling to heavier workloads on an as-needed basis.

Intelligent process automation (IPA) has more cognitive capabilities than RPA when used in conjunction with NLP, machine learning, computer vision, and other subfields.

Introduction to Computer Vision

With this brief understanding of all the related subfields of AI, you will now learn about computer vision, the prime purpose of this book. In this section, you will explore the basic concepts, building blocks, and algorithms of computer vision and learn how to implement them using the most up-to-date versions of OpenCV and Python.

Computer vision, also referred to as *vision*, is the recent cutting-edge field within computer science that deals with enabling computers, devices, or machines in general to see, understand, interpret, or manipulate what is being seen.

Computer vision technology implements deep learning techniques and in a few cases also employs NLP techniques as a natural progression of steps to analyze extracted text from images. With all the advancements of deep learning, building functions such as image classification, object detection, tracking, and image manipulation has become simpler and more accurate, thus leading way to exploring more complex autonomous applications such as self-driving cars, humanoids, and drones. With deep learning, we can now manipulate images, such as superimposing Tom Cruise's features onto another face or converting a picture into a sketch mode or watercolor painting mode. We can eliminate the background noise of a picture and highlight the subject in focus or take a stable picture even with the shakiest of hands. We can estimate the closeness, structure, and shape of objects, and we can estimate the textures of a surface too. With different lights or camera exposure, we can identify objects and recognize an object that we have seen before.

In computer vision, by saying we are enabling computers to "see," we mean enabling machines and devices to process digital visual data, which can include images taken with traditional cameras, a graphical representation of a location, a video, a heat intensity map of any data, and beyond.

As you can see, computer vision applications are becoming ubiquitous in our day-to-day lives. We can find an object or a face in a video or in a live video feed, understand motion and patterns within a video, and increase or decrease the size, brightness, or sharpness of an image.

Scope

To understand what constitutes computer vision, look at Figure 1-4.

Figure 1-4. *Image of a cricket game*

Though you are looking this image for the first time, you can probably tell that this image is of the sport cricket being played on a bright day. Specifically, it is a match between teams Australia and South Africa, and Australia won the match. The overall mood is that of celebration, and a few players can be named either by recognizing their facial features or by reading the names printed on their shirts.

The information you can observe is complex for a computer vision application; this could be a set of multiple inferences. Let's now map the whole human-driven interpretation to a machine's vision processes.

- You can observe objects such as grass/ground, people, cricket equipment advertisements, and sports uniforms. These objects are then grouped into categories. This process of extracting information is referred to as *image detection and classification*.

- At a high level, there is ground, and there is a pitch. While it is difficult to exactly pinpoint the boundaries of each, making the markings based on the objects within the image is possible. This process is referred to as *image segmentation*.

- Taking this to the next level, you can get smarter and smaller boundaries that can help identify specific people and objects in the image. This can be observed with small boxes marked around each potential unique object, as shown in Figure 1-5.

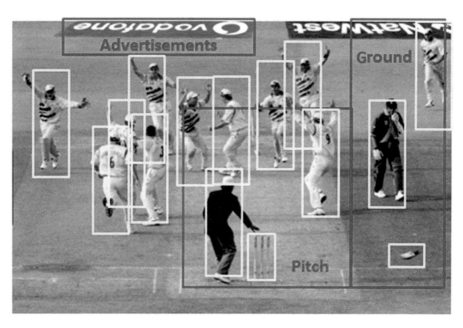

Figure 1-5. *Marking unique objects*

- Now, within each box, there could be people or different cricket-related objects. At the next level, you can detect and tag what each box contains, also shown in Figure 1-5. This process is called *object detection*.

- Extending this, you can look closely at the people's faces and through the face recognition process exactly determine who each player is. You also can observe that each person is of different height and build.

- Names on the back of the shirts of the players can be another source for determining who each player is. An optical character recognition (OCR) handwriting recognition process can recognize shapes and lines and infer letters or characters.

- Depending on the color of the uniform, you can infer what type of match it is and what teams are playing. Identifying the colors of the pixels is part of the image detection and manipulation process.

- In the process of playing the game, movement of the ball can be tracked and the speed at which the ball strikes the bat can be computed or determined. The path the ball will potentially take can be determined as well. A few important calculations such as how many ball serves have hit a particular spot on the pitch can be computed. This is possible using a process called *motion tracking.*

- Sometimes the determination of whether the player is "in" or "out" is determined by his leg position while the player is striking the ball. To accurately determine this, images from different cameras set up at different angles need to be analyzed to identify the accurate position of the player's leg. This process is called *image reconstruction*, where an object is compiled from different tomographic projects of the same object in different angles.

In Chapters 4, 5, and 6, we will cover all the processes listed here in detail with hands-on examples. In the next section, let's look at what makes computer vision a difficult and complex system to build.

Challenges of Computer Vision

Digital visual data sources can be webcams, cameras, video recorders, scanners, and others. The accuracy of computer vision applications is determined by how well the images or videos are interpreted. In this section, we will look at a few important aspects of images that can make the whole process of image interpretation complex.

- Illusions in an image can be confusing. For example, is Figure 1-6 representing two faces facing each other or a vase?

Figure 1-6. *Faces or vase?*

- There can be issues with camera sensors in low or bad light conditions. The images can get noisy or pixelated when zooming in (see Figure 1-7).

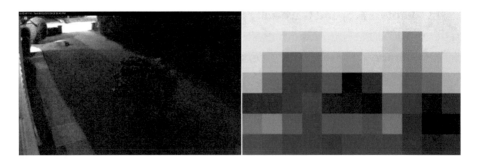

Figure 1-7. *Zooming in*

- The same object can look different from different angles. For example, Figure 1-8 shows the Eiffel Tower from different angles.

Figure 1-8. *Different angles*

- An object in motion can look different during the movement. For example, Figure 1-9 shows different images of a cheetah running.

Figure 1-9. *In motion*

- There can be background clutter that can make identifying the object of focus difficult.

- Finally, there can be many variations of the same object, such as different kinds of chairs.

Dealing with all these cases makes computer vision a hard problem to solve. In humans, the collection of data (through vision) happens constantly. Unlike with machines, there is a little chance that a human can misclassify a dog when seen in different positions.

Real-World Applications of Computer Vision

In this section, we will cover computer vision applications across domains such as automotive, healthcare and biomedical, and retail.

Automotive Industry

Computer vision has been in constant use since XXX in the automotive industry, especially to improve the safety and functionality of modern vehicles. Vehicles are equipped with sensors and cameras that can collect images and data regarding everything around the vehicle (see Figure 1-10). Thus, vehicles are able to detect speed limit signs on the road, warn or inform the driver when parked in a no-parking zone, proactively find an open parking space, and guide the driver to reach a location.

Proactive warnings or intimations regarding diversions, gas stations, hazardous obstacles, and so on, are just a few more examples.

Figure 1-10. *Computer vision in the automotive industry (source: Neuromation.io)*

The recent advent of self-driving cars has brought a revolution in the way intelligence can be built into automobiles to manage traffic congestion, road accidents, and proactive vehicle care.

Healthcare and Biomedical Industry

The healthcare and biomedical industry has seen an equal amount of adoption and traction for computer vision as the automobile industry.

In addition to advances in the way human organs and related data are photographed and stored, the way this data is interpreted and visualized has been drastically changed with computer vision algorithms. Preventive care is now possible for cancer and other genetic diseases because computers are able to detect potential occurrence in images from microscopes with very high precision. In addition, robots are able to perform complex surgeries with accuracy and efficiency.

In the case of surgeries, predicting the amount of blood loss is important because it can avoid unnecessary blood transfusions costing approximately $10 billion worldwide. Similarly, storing the analysis data and gaining insights from digital health reports of patients can help improve the accuracy and effectiveness of treatments.

Retail Industry

Both online and physical retail stores are extensively using computer vision to improve the customer experience, provide competitive alternatives, and optimize processes. Amazon, for example, implements computer vision to identify similar products that are marked at different prices and provide a comparison-based suggestion to customers as well as advice to sellers on positioning a particular product online. An Amazon Go store is a partially automated store with no checkout stations or cashiers that lets customers buy products of their choice, and payments are dealt with offline via their Amazon accounts.

Another example of an online retail store using computer vision is an eyewear store. Customers can simulate how specific frames look on their face or use a recommended design for a face type to help choose among the eyewear.

Images and Their Features

At the core of computer vision is its input, which is referred to as an *image*. Sources of images include cameras, video recorders, scanners, and microscopic images, among others. Let's now look at what images are, how are they stored and represented internally, and what image features can be used by vision algorithms to re-create, manipulate, analyze, track, and interpret images.

In simple technical terms, an *image* is a two-dimensional vector or a matrix with a finite number of rows and columns.

The following are different characteristics of images:

- The width of an image is represented by the number of columns in the matrix.

- The height of the image is represented by the number of rows in the matrix.

- An image is composed of multiple pixels, and a pixel is a core component of an image that is represented by one element in the matrix.

- The value in each pixel represents a channel that signifies a visual aspect of the image such as brightness, scale, color, and so on. The pixel values can take either a number between 0 and 255 or an RGB representation. A combination of these values then forms a color. The image thus formed is called a *three-channel* image.

The image features listed here (width, height, resolution, depth, and channels) are used in computer vision algorithms.

Color Spaces

The color space concept helps in storing and reproducing color schemes and hence is also called a *color model*. For example, in a grayscale color space, a pixel is represented as a single 8-bit unsigned integer value that corresponds to the brightness or gray intensity of that pixel. Figure 1-11 displays all the possible colors that exist within the grayscale color space.

Figure 1-11. *Grayscale color space*

The RGB color space has each pixel represented by three different 8-bit integer values that correspond to the red, green, and blue color intensity of that pixel. Figure 1-12 depicts how all other colors (such as yellow or pink) between the three main colors are formed.

Figure 1-12. *Other colors (such as yellow or pink)*

Another four-channel color space is the CMYK color space (representing cyan, maroon, yellow, and key/black). Figure 1-13 shows an example of the CMYK color space.

C component   M component   Y component   K component

Figure 1-13. *CMYK color space*

Overall, images are matrix-like structures that have features or properties such as height, width, channels, depth, element type, and so on. In the next section, let's look at the process flow for the computer vision process that covers where and how the input comes from, how the input is processed, and what the outcome is.

Core Building Blocks (Input – Process – Output)

The core process of a computer vision system involves receiving the input from sources such as cameras, smartphones, scanners, email attachments, printers, faxes, and so on, in the form of images or PDFs. The image or PDF data is extracted using image recognition or optical character recognition (OCR) or intelligent character recognition (ICR) engines (see Figure 1-14).

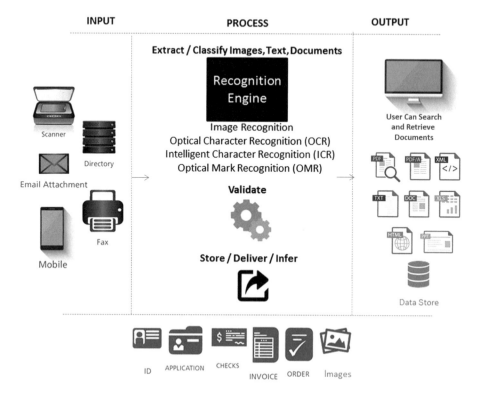

Figure 1-14. *Input – process – output*

For example, let's take a case of smartphone with a photo gallery application and a built-in camera that allows you to take pictures or videos. Take a photograph using the camera, apply a filter to enhance the photo, and email the file using an email application. While this may sound like a simple process, it internally uses critical functions of computer vision.

In this example, the images or documents can be provided by a wide range of input devices such as scanners, cameras, and so on. Just the way an image recognition engine extracts and classifies images, an OCR/ICR engine extracts and classifies text from images and documents.

Optical Character Recognition and Intelligent Character Recognition

Optical character recognition (OCR) is about recognizing scanned images that have textual content and translating images into text-searchable files. Converting an image to text files reduces the storage footprint and makes them more portable. Multiple neural network algorithms are used to poll the results and extract a final translated file. The input image is converted into a machine format that is interpretable by machines and then matched to a predefined code and a character. Once the image is converted into text, it becomes easy to manipulate based on the use case requirements.

As a next step, there's a need to recognize handwritten content, which is where *intelligent character recognition* (ICR) comes in. Since it has to deal with human/handwritten content, ICR is more complex than OCR. The character recognition process is more or less the same, but there needs to be some intelligence included to make the computer think like a human while interpreting the characters, thus mandating a built-in dictionary.

Optical Mark Recognition

Optical mark recognition (OMR) is similar to OCR and ICR but applies to slightly different use cases. This technology is used to compute scores in examinations.

Conclusion

In this chapter, we defined artificial intelligence and its subfields including robotics, intelligent process automation, expert systems, speech and voice recognition, machine learning (deep learning), and computer vision. We took a nontechnical approach to understanding what comprises computer vision, its application across domains, and its challenges. You learned about the core building blocks of computer vision and its functions. At the heart of computer vision is its core element, the image. We defined what an image is in the context of computer vision, what the key features are, and how an image is represented and stored as machine code.

In the next chapter, we will cover the open source computer vision library OpenCV. With hands-on code examples, we'll cover setting up OpenCV, working with Python libraries, and understanding the syntax and modules that help implement key computer vision functions.

CHAPTER 2

OpenCV with Python

This chapter will lay the foundations for learning computer vision algorithms through hands-on exercises using the most widely adopted open source computer vision framework, OpenCV 3.4.3 with Python 3.7. The chapter will cover setting up your system with OpenCV and the Python libraries, understanding key modules and out-of-box functions for computer vision implementations, and learning the syntax for scaling up.

Specifically, the following topics are covered in this chapter:

- Overview of OpenCV, its history, and its setup using the latest versions of OpenCV 3.4.3 and Python 3.7

- Introduction to the NumPy library and image-related functions

- How to create OpenCV projects

- Key modules for image access, manipulations, transformation, and tracking

© Sunila Gollapudi 2019
S. Gollapudi, *Learn Computer Vision Using OpenCV*,
https://doi.org/10.1007/978-1-4842-4261-2_2

About OpenCV

The name OpenCV comes from "open source computer vision."
The framework comprises tools, libraries, and modules that have
built-in support for implementing computer vision applications. It is one
of the most widely adopted toolkits with a strong developer community.
It is known for its scale of building real-world use cases for commercial use
as well. Version 3.4.3 of OpenCV, in conjunction with version 3.7 of Python,
is used for all the coding examples in this book. OpenCV supports the C/
C++, Python, and Java languages, and it can be used to build computer
vision applications for desktop and mobile operating systems alike,
including Windows, Linux, macOS, Android, and iOS. In this book, we will
focus on using it with Python on the Windows OS.

OpenCV started at Intel Research Lab during an initiative to advance
approaches for building CPU-intensive applications. It was conceived as a
way to make computer vision infrastructure universally available.

Setting Up OpenCV with Python

Let's set up OpenCV with Python.

Windows Installation

Follow these steps to install OpenCV on Windows:

1. Go to `https://www.python.org/downloads/windows/` to access the latest stable Python version for Windows (Python 3.7.0 in this book).

2. Download the executable for Windows with the required bit configuration and run it.

3. Click "Customize installation" (see Figure 2-1).

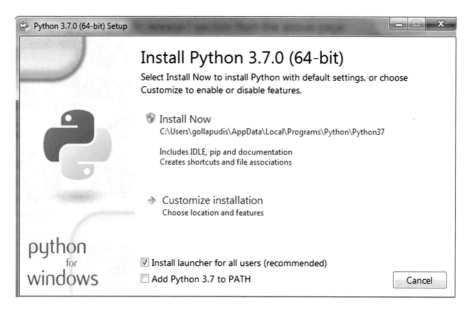

Figure 2-1. *Choosing to customize the installation*

4. Select the advanced options you want, set the path (if necessary), and click Install, as shown in Figure 2-2.

Figure 2-2. *Selecting advanced options*

5. Check that the setup was successful, as shown in Figure 2-3.

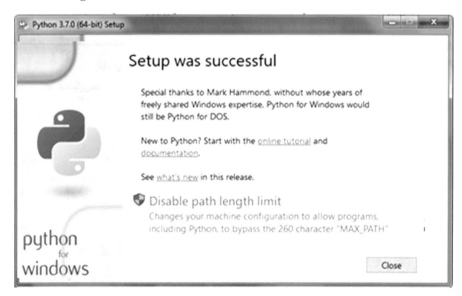

Figure 2-3. *Success!*

6. From the command prompt, type **python** to double-check that the installation was successful and verify the installed version, as shown in Figure 2-4.

```
C:\WINDOWS\system32\cmd.exe - python
Microsoft Windows [Version 6.1.7601]
Copyright (c) 2009 Microsoft Corporation.  All rights reserved.

C:\Users\gollapudis>python
Python 3.7.0 (v3.7.0:1bf9cc5093, Jun 27 2018, 04:59:51) [MSC v.1914 64 bit (AMD6
4)] on win32
Type "help", "copyright", "credits" or "license" for more information.
>>>
```

Figure 2-4. *Verifying the installation at the command line*

7. Download NumPy (the version used here is numpy-1.14.6+mkl-cp37-cp37m-win_amd64. whl) from https://www.lfd.uci.edu/~gohlke/pythonlibs/#numpy.

8. Download OpenCV version 3.4.3 (the version used here is opencv_python-3.4.3+contrib-cp37-cp37m-win_amd64.whl) from https://www.lfd. uci.edu/~gohlke/pythonlibs/#opencv.

9. Both the downloaded NumPy and OpenCV libraries will need to be placed in the Python installation folder. On the command prompt, navigate to the Python installation folder.

10. Install NumPy and OpenCV from the command prompt in the default Python location using the following commands:

    ```
    pip install "numpy-1.14.6+mkl-cp37-cp37m-win_
    amd64.whl"
    pip install "opencv_python-3.4.3+contrib-cp37-
    cp37m-win_amd64.whl"
    ```

35

11.   If the install was successful, you'll see the message shown in Figure 2-5 at the command prompt.

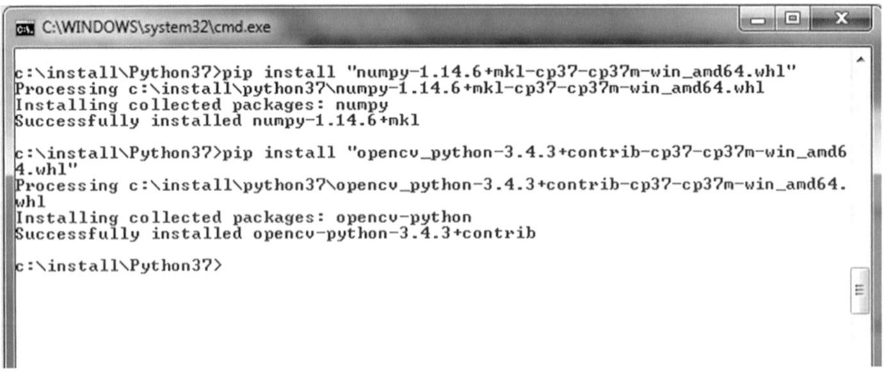

```
C:\WINDOWS\system32\cmd.exe

c:\install\Python37>pip install "numpy-1.14.6+mkl-cp37-cp37m-win_amd64.whl"
Processing c:\install\python37\numpy-1.14.6+mkl-cp37-cp37m-win_amd64.whl
Installing collected packages: numpy
Successfully installed numpy-1.14.6+mkl

c:\install\Python37>pip install "opencv_python-3.4.3+contrib-cp37-cp37m-win_amd6
4.whl"
Processing c:\install\python37\opencv_python-3.4.3+contrib-cp37-cp37m-win_amd64.
whl
Installing collected packages: opencv-python
Successfully installed opencv-python-3.4.3+contrib

c:\install\Python37>
```

Figure 2-5. *Successful install*

12.   To verify the installation is error-free, the following import commands on the Python editor should not throw any error:

```
>>import numpy
>>import cv2
```

13.   To check the installation version, run this:

```
>>print(cv2.__version__)
```

It should print 3.4.3.

macOS Installation

You can use Homebrew to install OpenCV and Python on macOS. Follow these steps:

1.   Install Python using the following command:

```
$ brew install python
```

2. Verify the Python installation using the following:

    ```
    $ which python
    ```

3. You should see /usr/local/bin/python printed on the terminal. This indicates that you are using "brewed Python." Open the terminal and run the following command:

    ```
    $ brew tap homebrew/science
    ```

4. Install NumPy.

    ```
    $ pip install numpy
    ```

5. Install OpenCV.

    ```
    $ brew install opencv --with-tbb --with-opengl
    ```

6. OpenCV is now installed on your machine, and you can find it at /usr/local/Cellar/opencv/3.4.3/.

7. Check the versions using this:

    ```
    $ cd /Library/Python/3.7/site-packages/
    $ ln -s /usr/local/Cellar/opencv/3.1.0/lib/
    python2.7/site-packages/cv.py
    cv.py
    $ ln -s /usr/local/Cellar/opencv/3.1.0/lib/
    python2.7/site-packages/cv2.so
    cv2.so
    ```

Using Modules

OpenCV consists of two types of modules, main and additional modules.

- **Main modules**: These modules are more or less the core modules of OpenCV and come by default with the packaged versions. They form core modules because they provide the core functionalities such as image-processing tasks, filtering, transformation, and others.

- **Extra modules**: These modules do not come by default with the OpenCV distribution. These modules are related to additional computer vision functionalities such as text recognition.

Table 2-1 describes the main modules.

Table 2-1. *Main Modules*

Module Name	Function or Purpose
core	Includes all core OpenCV functionalities such as basic structures, Mat classes, and so on.
imgproc	Includes image-processing features such as transformations, manipulations, filtering, and so on.
Imgcodecs	Includes functions for reading and writing images.
videoio	Includes functions for reading and writing videos.
highgui	Includes functions for GUI creation to visualize results.
video	Includes video analysis functions such as motion detection and tracking, the Kalman filter, and the infamous CAM Shift algorithm (used for object tracking).
calib3d	Includes calibration and 3D reconstruction functions that are used for the estimation of transformation between two images.

(continued)

Table 2-1. (*continued*)

Module Name	Function or Purpose
features2d	Includes functions for keypoint-detection and descriptor-extraction algorithms that are used in object detection and categorization algorithms.
objdetect	Supports object detection.
dnn	Used for object detection and classification purposes, among others. The dnn module is relatively new in the list of main modules and has support for deep learning.
ml	Includes functions for classification and regression and covers most of the machine learning capabilities.
flann	Supports optimized algorithms that deal with the nearest neighbor search of high-dimensional features in large data sets. FLANN stands for Fast Library for Approximate Nearest Neighbors (FLANN).
photo	Includes functions for photography-related computer vision such as removing noise, creating HD images, and so on.
stitching	Includes functions for image stitching that further uses concepts such as rotation estimation and image warping.
shape	Includes functions that deal with shape transformation, matching, and distance-related topics.
superres	Includes algorithms that handle resolution and enhancement.
videostab	Includes algorithms used for video stabilization.
viz	Display widgets in a 3D visualization window.

In addition to the modules in Table 2-1, OpenCV has modules based on CUDA (an API created by Nvidia). Using these modules is not covered in this book, but it is worth noting that these modules provide additional scale.

Working with Images and Videos

Images and videos that form the primary input to a computer vision application are represented in matrix format, as covered in Chapter 1. This matrix stores details of the images such as width, height, depth, channel, and others. You will first look at the C++ core class, or, module called Mat, which stands for "matrix." The Python equivalent is represented by numpy. ndarray. NumPy is a Python library that contains a wide set of numerical algorithms and mathematical operations that support working with large multidimensional arrays and matrices.

Using NumPy

Before working on the OpenCV libraries, you will first look at the NumPy library, including the data types, functions, and syntax to work with images.

Chapter 1 introduced images and their properties. NumPy facilitates a special *n*-dimensional array called ndarray that can hold image and related data. An *n*-dimensional array type is defined as numpy.ndarray.

The following is the code to create an *n*-dimensional array:

```
1  import numpy
2  newlist = [1,2,3]
3  type(newList)
4  newArray = np.array(newList)
5  type(newArray)
```

Line 1: Imports the NumPy library.

Line 2: Creates a new list object in Python. A list is represented by square braces, as in [and].

Line 3: Displays the object data type as list .

Line 4: Uses NumPy's array() function to create a new array using the existing list object. An array is represented within parentheses. So, this function creates an object called newArray that is an array initialized with a single row and three columns, represented as ([1,2,3]).

Line 5: Displays this new object as numpy.ndarray.

The zeros() or ones() function in NumPy libraries can be used to create an *n*-dimensional array. The following code helps create a 3×2 matrix initiated with zeros():

```
1   np.zeros(shape=(3,2))
2   np.ones((2,4))
```

The output of the previous lines is shown here:

```
array([[0.,0.], [0.,0.], [0.,0.]])
array([[1.,1.,1.,1.], [1.,1.,1.,1.]])
```

All ndarray functions that help extract and manipulate ndarray can be found at https://www.tutorialspoint.com/numpy/numpy_ndarray_object.htm.

Reading and Loading Images with OpenCV and NumPy

Create a folder called images in the Python home path and add a few images in JPG and PNG formats for examples. Add panda.jpg, as shown in Figure 2-6.

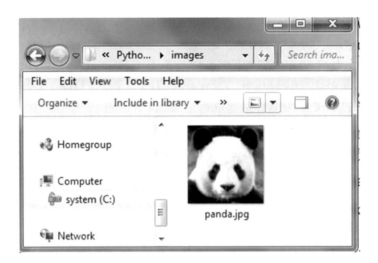

Figure 2-6. *Adding panda.jpg*

Try the following program to read, show, change the scale of, and write an image:

```
1  import numpy
2  import cv2
3
4  panda_image = cv2.imread("./images/panda.jpg")
5  panda_gray_image = cv2.cvtColor(panda_image, cv2.COLOR_
   BGR2GRAY)
6  cv2.imshow("Gray panda", panda_gray_image)
7  cv2.imshow("Color panda", panda_gray_image)
8  cv2.imwrite("gray_panda", panda_gray_image)
9  cv2.waitKey(0)
10 cv2.destroyAllWindows()
```

Line 1: Imports the NumPy library; this is important because the matrix format of the image is represented by the NumPy data type ndarray (an *n*-dimensional array).

Line 2: Imports the OpenCV library that gives access to all the functions to operate on images.

Line 4: Reads the image panda.jpg that was just placed in the images folder in Python's default path. This line reads the image and stores it in a variable called panda_image.

Try printing the data type of the image that is read using type(panda_image). It should show numpy.ndarray. This is just for verification.

Line 5: Converts the image to grayscale, and using the method cvtColor, passes the constant COLOR_BGR2GRAY and stores it in another variable, called panda_gray_image.

Lines 6 and 7: Display both the images in a window using the imshow() method. The first attribute for this method is the window name (see Figure 2-7).

Figure 2-7. *First attribute of method showing window name*

Line 8: Saves the converted image into a folder using the imwrite() method.

The folder will now have a new JPG saved (see Figure 2-8).

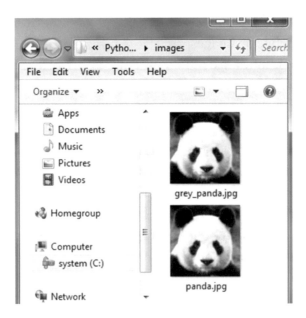

Figure 2-8. *Saving new JPG*

Line 9: Gives 0 ms before keystroke action.

Line 10: Closes all the windows.

Working with a Histogram Representation

There is another representation for images, and that is a *histogram.*

```
1   import numpy as np
2   import cv2
3
4   from matplotlib import pyplot as plt
5
6   image = cv2.imread("./images/panda.jpg")
7   #plot a histogram
8   histogram_image = cv2.calaHist([Image], [0], done, [256],
    [0,256])
9   #flaten the histogram
```

```
10  plt.hist(histogram_image.ravel(), 256, [0,256])
11  plt.show()
12  #view color channels
13  color = ['b','g','r']
14
15  #seperate the colors and plot the histogram
16  for I, col in enumaerate(color):
17      hist = cv2.calcHist([image], [i], None, [256], [0,256])
18      plt.plot(hist, color = col)
19      plt.xlim([0.256])
20
21  plt.show ()
```

Line 1: Imports the NumPy library. This is important as the matrix format of the image is represented by the NumPy data type ndarray (*n*-dimensional array).

Line 2: Imports the OpenCV library that gives access to all the functions to operate on images.

Line 4: Imports matplotlib, which has libraries for plotting a histogram.

Line 6: Reads the image panda.jpg that was just placed in the images folder in Python's default path. This line reads the image and stores it in a variable called image.

Line 8: Generates a histogram of the image that is loaded.

Line 10: Flattens the histogram.

Lines 16 through 19: Loops the values on the flattened histogram, separates the colors, and plots the data.

Line 21: Displays the histogram.

Figure 2-9 shows the output of the previous program for the panda image.

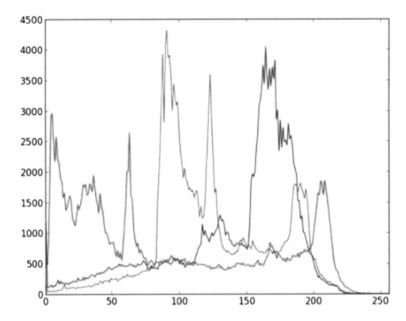

Figure 2-9. Histogram

Videos

In the section, you will learn about loading videos from a webcam or a file stored at a location. You will load a video frame by frame and also save it to another video file.

Loading Videos from a Webcam

Here is how to load a video from a webcam:

```
1  import cv2
2  import numpy as np
3
4  cap = cv2.VideoCapture(0)
5
6  while True:
7      ret, frame = cap.read()
```

```
 8
 9        cv2.imshow("frame", frame)
10
11        key = cv2.waitKey(1)
12        if key == 27:
13            break
14
15  cap.release()
16  cv2.destroyAllWindows()
```

Lines 1 and 2: Import the OpenCV and NumPy libraries.

Line 4: Loads frames from a webcam using the VideoCapture() method. The parameter 0 indicates the first webcam, and the number can change if there is more than one webcam.

Lines 6 through 13: Read through video frames.

A video is just a sequence of images, and you need to loop (using a while loop) through images. Each frame from the video is read using the read() method.

The r parameter takes a value of true or false. It's true if cap is reading a frame based on the completion of reading the images. Then the image is shown using the imshow() method. The waitkey() method is used to wait until you press the key.

Lines 15 and 16: Clear the stream and close the window.

Loading Videos from a File

Here is how to load a video from a file:

```
1  import cv2
2  import numpy as np
3
4  mountains_video = cv2.VideoCapture("mountains.mp4")
5
```

```
 6  while True:
 7          ret, frame = mountains_video.read()
 8
 9          cv2.imshow("frame", frame)
10
11          key = cv2.waitKey(25)
12          if key == 27:
13              break
14
15  mountains_video.release()
16  cv2.destroyAllWindows()
```

Line 1 and 2: Import the OpenCV and NumPy libraries.

Line 4: Loads frames from a webcam using the VideoCapture() method; the parameter will be the video file name.

Lines 6 through 13: Read through video frames.

A video is just a sequence of images, and you need to loop (using a while loop) through images. Each frame from the video is read using the read() method.

r takes a value of true or false. It's true if cap is reading a frame based on the completion of reading the images. Then the image is shown using the imshow() method. The waitkey() method is used to wait until you press the key.

Lines 15 and16: Clear the stream and close the window.

Reading the Video and Writing into a File

The same code is used to read the video and write to a file, except when each frame is read, a new parameter holds the read frame in a flip mode and writes the flipped frame into another video file.

```
1  import cv2
2  import numpy as np
```

```
 3
 4  mountains_video = cv2.VideoCapture("mountains.mp4")
 5
 6  fcc = cv2.VideoWriter_fourcc(*"XVID")
 7  out = cv2.VideoWriter("new_mountains.avi", fcc, 28, (640, 360))
 8
 9  while True:
10      ret, f = mountains_video.read()
11      f2 = cv2.flip(f, 1)
12
13      cv2.imshow("frame2", f2)
14      cv2.imshow("frame", f)
15
16      out.write(f2)
17
18      key = cv2.waitKey(20)
19      if key == 27:
20          break
21
22  out.release()
23  mountains_video.release()
24  cv2.destroyAllWindows()
```

Conclusion

In this chapter, you learned about the OpenCV framework and how it works in conjunction with Python libraries. You reviewed the core and advanced modules of OpenCV. You learned the functions for reading, writing, showing, and saving images and videos.

In the next chapter, you will learn about relevant deep learning algorithms that power computer vision, about some specific complex problems that they solve, and about how they can be implemented using OpenCV modules.

CHAPTER 3

Deep Learning for Computer Vision

The goal of this chapter is to introduce you to the underlying deep learning algorithms that power computer vision applications. Deep learning is applied in the classification, detection, segmentation, and generation of images and videos in computer vision applications. This chapter will cover the methods to train deep learning models and deploy them on various platforms. The following are the topics covered in this chapter:

- Understanding the basics and taxonomy of deep learning

- Convergence areas of deep learning and computer vision

- A recap of neural networks and common terms used in deep learning techniques

- Step-by-step guide to how convolution and recurrent neural networks work and how they are used in specific vision examples

© Sunila Gollapudi 2019
S. Gollapudi, *Learn Computer Vision Using OpenCV*,
https://doi.org/10.1007/978-1-4842-4261-2_3

Deep Learning: An Overview

Chapter 1 introduced machine learning and deep learning. In this chapter, you will take a deep dive into a few deep learning algorithms that power computer vision.

Deep learning is a subset of machine learning that focuses on learning significant features from the input data, especially in cases where the data is complex. This is more or less a replacement for a typical feature extractor that was built to be unique to complex data types such as images, videos, and so on. In Chapter 1, you learned some of the challenges of images and videos that can make the computer vision process overall a complex problem to solve. Applying some deep learning techniques such as convolution neural networks addresses these challenges seamlessly.

Traditional or elementary machine learning techniques were originally in use for computer vision. The K-nearest neighbor (KNN) technique and linear classifier are the most popular traditional approaches. With the KNN algorithm, each image is matched against all the images in the training data, and the image (or images) with the least distance measured is chosen to help classify the input image. In cases where an image had the same object with a different illumination or angle, the distance measure practically failed. Similarly, with the traditional linear classifier technique, each pixel value of the input image is assessed and tagged if it can be a parameter for matching. Typically, a weighted average value of the pixel is taken for comparison, which is why all the challenging areas of images (such as illuminations, different angles or image viewpoints, noise, background clutter, and multiple varieties of same objects) cause the algorithm to fail to match the input image.

Other more sophisticated techniques fail to match the output that deep learning techniques can match. Let's first look at what vision requirements are addressed by deep learning techniques before learning how they work.

Deep Learning Applications in Computer Vision

Computer vision enables the properties of human vision on a computer. A computer here could be a smartphone, drone, CCTV, MRI scanner, and so on, with various sensors for perception. The sensor produces images in a digital form that has to be interpreted by the computer. The basic building block of such interpretation or intelligence is explained in the next section. The different problems that arise in computer vision can be effectively solved using deep learning techniques.

Classification

Image classification is the task of labeling the whole image with an object or concept with confidence. The applications include identifying gender given an image of a person's face, identifying the type of pet, tagging photos, and so on. Figure 3-1 shows the output of such a classification task.

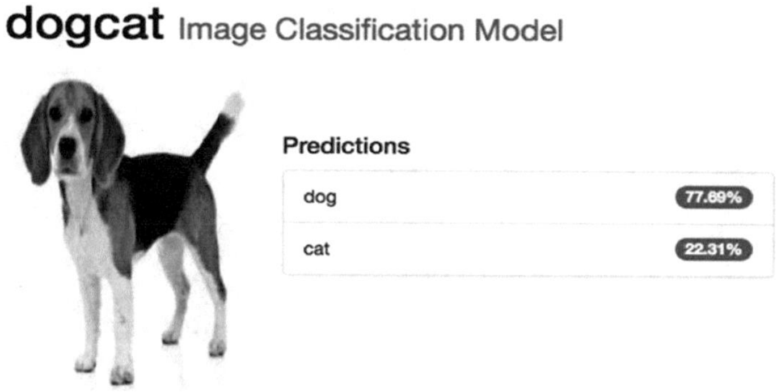

dogcat Image Classification Model

Predictions

| dog | 77.69% |
| cat | 22.31% |

Figure 3-1. *Output of classification task*

Detection and Localization

Detection or *localization* is an activity that involves finding an object and marking or boxing it. This has many real-world applications, especially in the automotive industry where self-driving cars detect objects through their camera sensors. The first image in Figure 3-2 depicts object detection, and the second image shows localization.

Figure 3-2. *Object detection and localization*

(Semantic) Segmentation

Segmentation is the process of doing pixel-wise classification. This gives a fine separation of objects, as shown in Figure 3-3. It is useful for processing medical images and satellite imagery.

Figure 3-3. *Segmentation*

Similarity Learning

Similarity learning is the process of learning how two images are similar. A score can be computed between two images based on the semantic meaning.

There are several applications of this, from finding similar products to performing facial identification.

Image Captioning

Image captioning is the task of describing an image with text, as shown in Figure 3-4.

Figure 3-4. *Captioning*

Generative Models

Generative models are interesting because they generate images. Figure 3-5 shows an example of a style transfer application where an image is generated with the content of that image and the style of other images. Specifically, it shows how an image of a temple uses the style of a pencil sketch.

Figure 3-5. *Generative modeling*

Images can be generated for other purposes such as new training examples, super-resolution images, and so on.

Video Analysis

Video analysis processes a video as a whole, as opposed to images. It has several applications, such as sports tracking, intrusion detection, and surveillance cameras.

Before we go deeper into the convolution and recurring neural network techniques of deep learning, let's quickly recap what neural networks are.

Neural Networks at Their Core

Let's look at a simple problem in Figure 3-6; the requirement is to recognize the objects from the handwritten script and image.

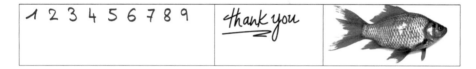

Figure 3-6. *Handwritten script and object*

For humans, this is not a big deal; they are recognized as the numbers 123456789, the text *thank you*, and the image of a goldfish. While this appears simple, it hides the complexity of the human brain. The brain can interpret these images incrementally, and this is done by visual cortices. Each cortex contains millions of neurons that are interconnected, enabling this interpretation.

If a computer program has to crack this recognition of digits, text, and images, how should that work? Should there be rules that help identify and differentiate one image from another?

Artificial Neural Networks

The research in neural networks started as an attempt to simulate multilayered learning. This definitely requires feeding input to the model a large amount of input variations of handwritten digits or text or object images from which the interpretation rules can be inferred and applied for prediction on a new image input.

Deep learning is an assemblage of techniques from an artificial neural network (ANN), which is a subfield of machine learning. As mentioned, ANNs are modeled on the human brain, which has multiples nodes that are linked and can pass information within them using the links. In the following sections, let's look at some core building blocks of ANNs.

Artificial Neurons or Perceptrons

Artificial neurons are called that because they emulate biological neurons and are structured as shown in Figure 3-7. These are the basic unit of computation in the neural network.

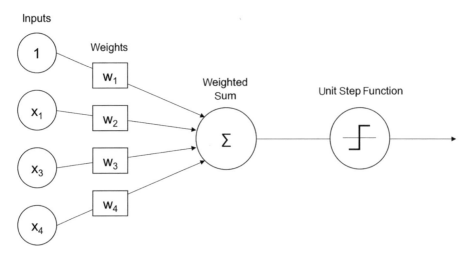

Figure 3-7. *Artificial neurons*

The following are the features and functions of artificial neurons:

- Each artificial neuron receives input from other neurons, and each of these inputs is associated with a *weight* (w) that is an indication of relative importance with the other inputs.

- These inputs set the context and activate the neurons by applying nonlinear or linear functions. These functions are called *step* or *activation* functions.

- An output transmitter transfers signals, also called *activations*, of the neurons.

- A core processing unit produces the output signals or activations from the input signals.

There is a process called *idealization* for a neuron, which refers to models that further allow inferencing. When more complexities are added to the model, the more robust the model gets.

The earlier step or activation functions add nonlinear aspects to the output of the neuron. This is required as this is what makes the whole output closer to being real because most real-world data is usually nonlinear.

These activation functions (or nonlinearity) take a single input and run mathematical operations on it. Table 3-1 describes different types of activation functions.

Table 3-1. *Activation Functions*

Type of Function	Description	Representation
Sigmoid	It converts the input value to a range between 0 and 1. Example: $\sigma(x) = 1 / (1 + \exp(-x))$	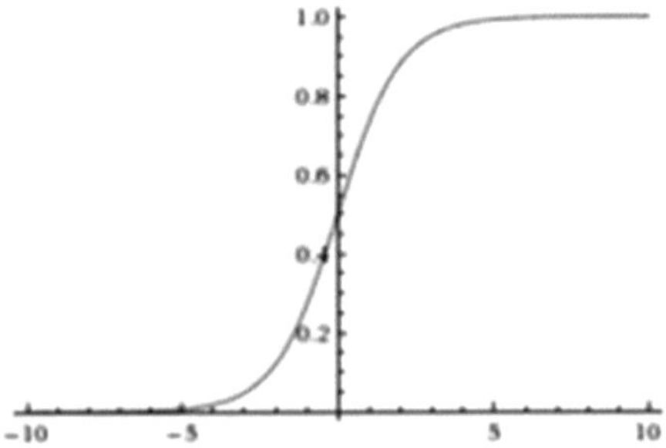
tanh	It converts the input value to a range between -1 and 1. Example: $\tanh(x) = 2\sigma(2x) - 1$	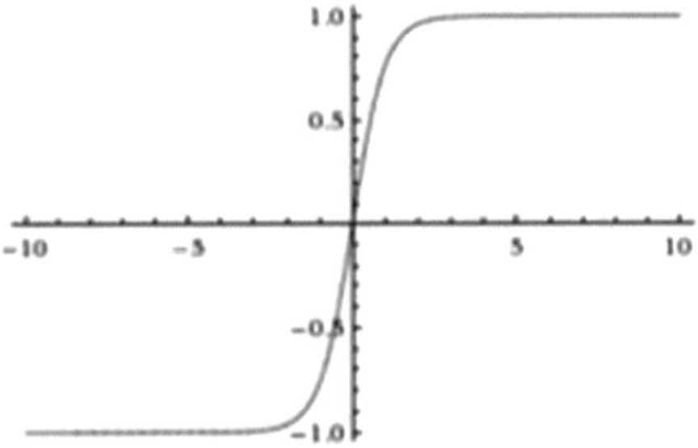
Rectified linear unit (ReLU)	It thresholds the input value at zero by replacing the negative numbers with zero. Example: $f(x) = \max(0, x)$	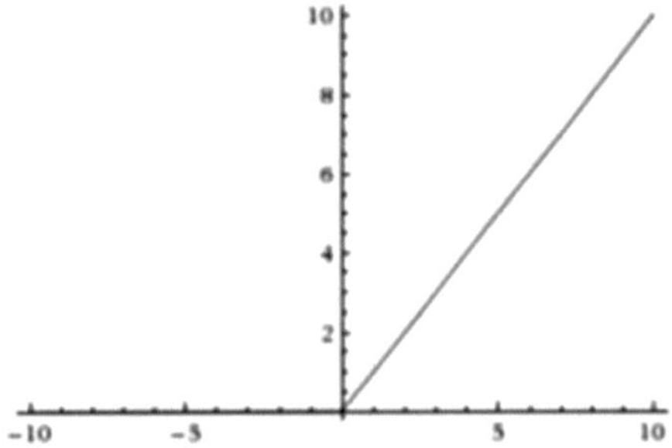

Figure 3-8 illustrates a typical structure of an ANN. Each circle in the diagram represents a neuron. The input layer pushes input values; the hidden layers of neurons then take the values as input. It is possible to have multiple layers within these hidden layers, where the output from one layer is fed as an input to the next layer. Each of these layers can be responsible for specialized learning. The last hidden layers feed into the output layer. The concept of the *credit assignment path* (CAP) refers to the path from input to output.

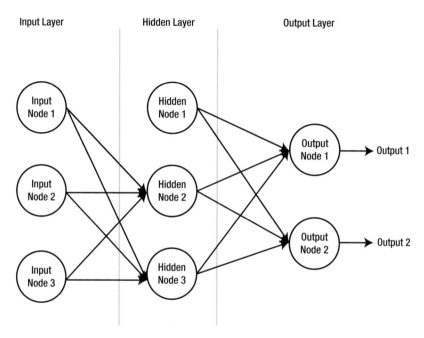

Figure 3-8. *Typical structure of an ANN*

In feedforward networks, the length of the path is the total number of hidden layers along with the output layer. These networks can be either single-layered or multiple-layered networks. Figure 3-8 shows a feedforward neural network with a single hidden layer. In the case of multiple hidden layers, each of the hidden layers is connected internally. The hidden layers are considered *hidden* because they are internally connecting the input and output layers and have no direct connection with the external world.

Training Neural Networks

The key to the highest accuracy or success of a deep learning algorithm is determined by how well the ANNs are trained. Training an ANN is complex because there is a need to optimize multiple parameters. Through a process called *backpropagation*, the input weights are adjusted based on the input relevance computed at each layer.

Backpropagation

A backpropagation algorithm is commonly used for training artificial neural networks. The weights are updated from backward based on the error calculated in a layer. Figure 3-9 shows the input navigation and weight computations transmitted backward.

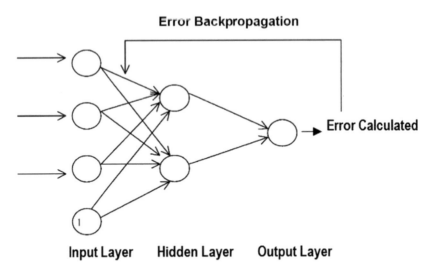

Figure 3-9. *Backpropagation*

After calculating the error, a gradient descent method can be applied to recalculate the weight.

Gradient Descent and Stochastic Gradient Descent

The gradient descent algorithm is responsible for accomplishing the multidimensional optimization until the global maximization is achieved. Gradient descent is a popular optimization technique used in many machine learning models. It is used to improve, or optimize, the model prediction. A variation of gradient descent called *stochastic gradient descent* (SGD) is becoming one of the most adopted methods. Optimization involves calculating the error value and changing the weights to achieve that minimal error. The direction of finding the minimum is the negative of the gradient of the loss function.

The learning rate determines how big each step should be. Note that ANNs with nonlinear activations will have local minima. SGD works better in practice for optimizing nonconvex cost functions.

In the next section, you will learn about two important neural network variations, convolution neural networks (CNNs) and recurrent neural networks (RNNs), that are heavily used in computer vision algorithms.

Convolutional Neural Networks

Convolution neural networks, also known as *convolution nets*, are a variation of regular neural networks.

The traditional approaches discussed earlier fail to solve the vision tasks when there are vast variations in images. Convolution neural networks solve the problem as they model smaller pieces of information and combine them using deep networks. This processing happens across multiple layers. The first layer applies *edge detection*, which refers to detecting edges and build templates. The next layers use these templates for the base, take simpler shapes from the image, and form more templates that include different object scales, positions, or illuminations. The last layers match the input images with all the templates, and the final output is a weighted sum of all the outputs. This helps handle complex variations in images with higher accuracy.

CNNs have three types of layers.

- Convolution layer

- Pooling layer

- Fully connected layer

CNNs work differently when compared to regular neural networks. In CNNs, the layers are set as three dimensions: height, width, and depth.

The neurons of one hidden layer connect only to a partial set of neurons of the other layer and don't connect to every neuron. Additionally, the output is reduced to a single vector of probability scores, organized along the depth dimension.

The hidden layers help in feature extraction; this is done by the convolution and pooling layers, and the final classification is done by the fully connected layer.

Convolution Layer

The convolution layer consists of spatial filters that are convolved along the spatial dimensions and summed up along the depth dimension of the input volume. The convolution layer is a key building block of a CNN. *Convolution* means combining two functions to produce a third function and using merging techniques. The convolution is done by applying a filter or kernel that helps form a feature map. The filter is applied on the different areas of the input, a matrix multiplication is done, and the summation of the matrices forms the feature map.

The term *stride* represents the pixel distance that each filter application uses. For example, a stride value of 1 indicates applying the filter/kernel at a 1-pixel distance. Padding is added to the feature map that is extracted. This is usually a layer of 0-value pixels to prevent the feature map from shrinking.

The final matrix that is formed by this function is passed through an activation function to make it nonlinear. This could be a ReLU activation function.

Pooling Layer

A pooling layer is added after the convolution layer. The pooling layer is responsible for reducing the dimensionality and thus reducing the parameter count to control the training timing and avoid overfitting.

A max pooling technique is the most common technique applied. This takes the maximum value in each window. This helps optimize the feature map size, ensuring key information about the image is retained.

So, the following are the key parameters in CNNs that decide on the optimization of the feature map:

- Kernel size

- Filter count

- Stride and

- Padding

Fully Connected Layer

After the convolution and pooling, the final feature map used for the "classification" task is executed by the fully connected layer. These fully connected layers can accept only one-dimensional data. Hence, the 3D data needs to be converted to 1D. For this, the standard Python flatten functions can be used. Neurons in the fully connected layer have full connections to all the activations in the previous layer, and they work exactly the way regular neural networks do.

CNNs are widely used for the image recognition, object detection, and tracking tasks of computer vision. The OpenCV functions internally implement CNN algorithms. You'll learn more about these implementations in the upcoming chapters.

Recurrent Neural Networks

Recurrent neural networks are key algorithms for handling sequential data. They are extensively used by Apple's Siri and Google's Voice Search. The key differentiating factor for RNN is that it can remember the input because it has internal memory. It is one of the key algorithms behind the scenes of the amazing achievements of deep learning in the past few years.

RNN is considered to be one of the most robust neural network algorithms. This is a relatively old algorithm but is becoming more popular in recent years because of the invention of long short-term memory (LSTM). Because of this, RNNs can remember some key information about the input and thus can be more accurate in predicting what is coming next.

Sequential data is handled very well. An example of sequential data is time-series data. Hence, this algorithm can be potentially effective in speech, text, financial data, audio, video, and weather analysis, among other domains. A stronger understanding of the sequence of steps can be established. This is not quite possible with other algorithms. In RNNs, unlike a feedforward neural network, the information is fed cyclically in loop. So, when a decision is made, both the current input and the learnings from the inputs received previously are used. Figure 3-10 shows the cyclic inputs in an RNN.

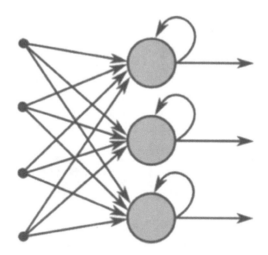

Figure 3-10. *Cyclic inputs in an RNN*

Usually an RNN has a short-term memory, but in conjunction with LSTM, it can have long-term memory as well. A recurrent neural network is able to remember exactly that because of its internal memory. It produces output, copies that output, and loops it back into the network. RNNs thus can add the immediate past to the present.

Input weights are added to both present and past inputs for RNNs. RNNs can map one to many, many to many (translation), and many to one (classifying a voice), as shown in Figure 3-11.

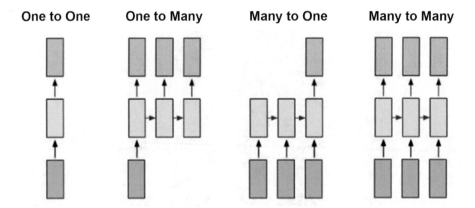

Figure 3-11. Mapping

Furthermore, they tweak their weights both through gradient descent and through backpropagation through time. Let's now look at how that happens.

Backpropagation Through Time

Backpropagation through time (BPTT) does backpropagation on an "unrolled" recurrent neural network. *Unrolling* is a visualization and conceptual tool to check on what is flowing through the network. This process is usually taken care of internally by the framework that is used to implement the RNN. LSTM networks are an extension for recurrent neural networks, and they basically extend the memory of RNNs. Therefore, BPTT is well suited to learn from important experiences that have long time lags in between.

The units of an LSTM are used as building units for the layers of an RNN, which is then often called an LSTM network.

Conclusion

In this chapter, you learned about deep learning, how convolution and recurrent neural networks work, and how you can train neural networks using backpropagation and related functions to compute weights for the inputs. The chapter then covered some key computer vision use cases that use deep learning algorithms. Finally, the chapter concluded with the modules in OpenCV that support deep learning algorithm implementations.

This chapter lays the foundation for the upcoming chapters, which cover the hands-on implementation of OpenCV modules with Python for image processing, object detection, and motion analysis and tracking real-world use cases.

CHAPTER 4

Image Manipulation and Segmentation

Chapters 4, 5, and 6 cover hands-on implementations for image manipulation, segmentation, object detection, and motion analysis and tracking along with a few real-world use cases. A brief introduction of these concepts was already given in Chapter 1, so these chapters will take you deeper into the implementation specifics. This chapter, specifically, covers image manipulations and segmentation-related functions that are core to image processing in computer vision applications. For each of the use cases, the chapter will show the Python syntax and implementations of the built-in functions in OpenCV.

The following topics are covered in this chapter:

- The chapter will give an overview of image manipulation and segmentation and the libraries that support these features.

- As part of image manipulations, the chapter will provide a step-by-step guide on how to perform transformations on images such as translations, rotations, resizing, blurring, sharpening, edge detection, masking, converting a photograph into a sketch, and more.

© Sunila Gollapudi 2019
S. Gollapudi, *Learn Computer Vision Using OpenCV*,
https://doi.org/10.1007/978-1-4842-4261-2_4

- As part of image segmentation, the chapter will cover how to partition an image into different regions using contour approximation; how to detect specific shapes such as lines, circles, and blobs; and how to identify the occurrence of a specific object or shape within an image.

- All implementations (including the libraries, functions, syntax, and hands-on code) are explained using OpenCV and Python.

Image Manipulations

Chapter 1 introduced what images are, their different properties, and their storage structure. You also learned how to read, show, and write images; change their color; and work with color spaces.

As a quick recap of what was covered in Chapter 1, images are stored in a two-dimensional (2D) matrix. You learned how to load, display, and show them within in a window. When an image is stored as a matrix, each cell represents a pixel. The pixels store a value that represents information about the image. For example, in the case of a grayscale image, the pixels store an integer value between 0 and 255. Changing the value of a pixel thus changes the image. This manipulation at a pixel level can be done by accessing a single pixel or a range of pixels in the image. Images can also be represented as histograms, and you have already looked at how to represent access and manipulate a few properties.

Overall, *image manipulation* refers to a process of altering or modifying an image for different purposes such as beautifying images, sharpening images with noise, restoring old black-and-white images and re-creating them in color, and so on.

Let's now start looking at various image manipulation requirements and how to implement each of them.

Accessing and Manipulating Pixels

In this section, you will write OpenCV/Python code to access the pixels in an image and modify the color of them.

The following Python code demonstrates how to access a pixel in an image and print it. Also, you can change the color of one pixel or a range of pixels.

Lines 1 through 5: These are common code lines that load the NumPy and OpenCV libraries and then load an image that is placed in a specific directory path using the imread() function.

```
1   import numpy
2   import cv2
3
4   #read the flower image and load it into a variable flower_image
5   flower_image=cv2.imread("./images/flower_pink.jpg")
6
7   #access a specific pixel using the coordinate based access
    from the matrix
8   pixel=flower_image[200,250]
9
10  #see what color space this pixel represents - this is an
    RBG representation
11  print(pixel)
12
13  #lets change the pixel color value to blue
14  flower_image[200,250]=(255,0,0)
15
16  #lets change the pixel color value to blue in a region
    range as against
17  flower_image[200:250,200:350]=(0,255,0)
18
19  cv2.imshow('modified pixel', flower_image)
20  cv2.waitkey(0)
```

Lines 8 and 11: Access a specific pixel by choosing the pixel coordinates and print the color representation in RGB values.

Line 14: Changes a specific pixel color to blue with the output shown in Figure 4-1.

Figure 4-1. *Changing one pixel*

Line 16: Picks a range of pixels and colors them green. The output shown in Figure 4-2 is the result of executing this line. (You can comment line 14 to see the output for this code.)

Figure 4-2. *Changing pixels to green*

Drawing Geometric Shapes or Writing Text on a Color Image

In this section, you will explore a few geometric functions in OpenCV. You can use the line(), rectangle(), circle(), ellipse(), polygon(), or putText() functions in OpenCV. Let's start with the tree shown in Figure 4-3 to draw or write text.

Figure 4-3. *No text yet*

The functions and syntax are as follows:

- `cv2.line()`: To draw a line, this function takes the following arguments:

    a. Image object on which the line needs to be drawn

    b. Starting point's pixel coordinates

    c. Ending point's pixel coordinates

    d. Color in BGR (not RGB) format

    e. Thickness (in pixels)

- `cv2.rectangle()`: To draw a square or rectangle, similar to the `line()` function, this function takes the following arguments:

    a. Image object on which the rectangle needs to be drawn

    b. Pixel coordinates of the vertex at the top left

    c.   Pixel coordinates of the lower-right vertex

    d.   Color in BGR (not RGB)

    e.   Thickness (in pixels)

- `cv2.circle()`: To draw a circle, this function takes the following arguments:

      a.   Image object on which the circle needs to be drawn

      b.   Center pixel's coordinates

      c.   Pixel radius of the circle

      d.   Color in BGR (not RGB)

      e.   Thickness (in pixels)

- `cv2.ellipse()`: To draw a ellipse, this function takes the following arguments:

      a.   Image object on which the ellipse needs to be drawn

      b.   Center pixel's coordinates

      c.   Length of the minor and major axes

      d.   Rotation angle of the ellipse (calculated counterclockwise)

      e.   Starting angle (calculated clockwise)

      f.   Final angle (calculated clockwise)

      g.   Color in BGR (not RGB—be careful)

      h.   Thickness

- `cv2.polyline()`: To draw a polygon, this function takes the following arguments:

      a.   Image object on which the polygon needs to be drawn

      b.   The image object on which to draw

     c.   The array of coordinates

     d.   True, if it is a closed line

     e.   Color

     f.   Thickness

- `cv2.putText()`: To write text, this function takes the following arguments:

  a.   The image on which the text is to be written

  b.   The text to be written

  c.   Coordinates of the text's starting point

  d.   Font to be used

  e.   Font size

  f.   Text color

  g.   Text thickness

  h.   The type of line used

```
1   import numpy
2   import cv2
3
4   #read the flower image and load it into a variable flower_image
5   flower_image=cv2.imread("./images/flower_pink.jpg")
6
7   cv2.line(flower_image,(25,21),(100,100),(255,0,0),5)
8   cv2.rectangle(flower_image,(25,21),(200,200),(0,255,0),2)
9   cv2.circle(flower_image,(50,50),50,(0,0,255),-1)
10
11  cv2.imshow("Geometry",flower_image)
12  cv2.waitKey(0)
```

The previous Python program creates the output shown in Figure 4-4.

Figure 4-4. *Output*

Filtering Images

Image filtering is a mechanism to modify an image and extract or highlight the detail that is useful for further computer vision tasks. Filtering processes can include adding or removing noise in an image, removing the background or a specific object, extracting edges, and blurring or sharpening an image. When photographs are taken in sunlight, there would be a few bright and dark areas; likewise, a photograph taken at night would have noise. Even images with too many colors can be categorized as noise. In this section, you will learn how to implement filtering using the built-in OpenCV libraries.

Figure 4-5 is an example of "salt and pepper" noise.

Figure 4-5. *Salt and pepper noise*

Let's now look at how to add or remove noise from an image. You will use the median filter for removing salt and pepper noise. This filter uses the same technique of neighborhood filtering; the key technique in this is the use of a median value. The workflow of neighborhood filtering is covered in the following example. As such, this filter is nonlinear by nature.

This filter takes the median value of all the pixels in the neighborhood pixel region and replaces the pixels in context with the median value. This removes random peak values in the region, which can be due to noise like salt and pepper noise. There is a typical kernel size that can be set. The higher the kernel value, the more effective the removal of the noise, with a side effect of having the blur in the image increase.

Here is the OpenCV function:

cv2.medianBlur(src, ksize[, dst])

This function smoothens an image using the median filter with the **ksize × ksize** aperture. Each channel of a multichannel image is processed independently.

The following Python code uses the medianBlur() function with a kernel value of 3. This means a 3 × 3 matrix of pixels around a pixel is taken, and the median of all the pixel values is used to replace that pixel.

```
1   import numpy
2   import cv2
3
4   #read the flower image and load it into a variable image
5   image=cv2.imread("./images/input1.jpg")
```

```
 6
 7  #kernel value of 3 3x3 matrix neighbourhood is used
 8  noisereduced_version = cv2.medianBlur(image,3)
 9
10  cv2.imshow("Original",image)
11  cv2.imshow("Corrected",noisereduced_version)
12
13  cv2.waitKey(0)
```

Let's simulate how the previous code converts or removes the salt and pepper noise. Consider the image matrix shown in Figure 4-6. Around the pixel value 6, a 3 × 3 pixel matrix is highlighted. When all these pixel values are placed in ascending order, it looks like this: 1, 1, 2, 2, 2, 2, 3, 5. The median for this list is 2. So, the final output of the pixel value 6 is replaced with 2. This process is repeated for each pixel value.

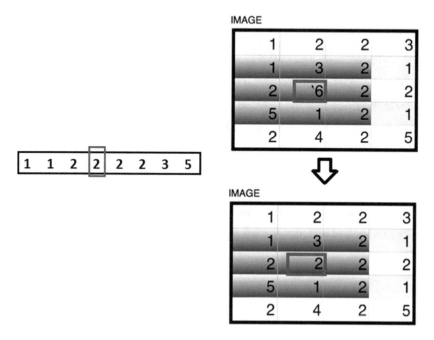

Figure 4-6. *3 × 3 pixel matrix highlighted*

The output image sample for a 3 × 3 kernel matrix is shown in Figure 4-7. The higher the kernel value, the lower the noise and the higher the blur.

Figure 4-7. *Output image sample for a 3 × 3 kernel matrix*

There are many more filtering functions such as bilateral filters, box filters, and Gaussian blur filters that are categorized as linear or nonlinear filters.

Transforming Images

Transformation operations on an image are usually referred to as *geometric transformations* applied on a photo. There are several other kinds of transformations as well, but this section will cover geometric transformations. These consist of, but are not limited to, shifting an image, rotating an image along an axis, and projecting it onto different planes.

There are two types of transformations: affine and nonaffine. Translation, resizing, and rotation are categorized as affine transformations of an image, and the warpAffine() function is used (see Figure 4-8).

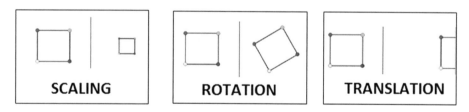

Figure 4-8. *Affine transformations*

The nonaffine transformations are also called *projective transformations.* This type of transformation does not preserve parallelism or length or angle of an image. The example in Figure 4-9 shows a nonaffine transformation.

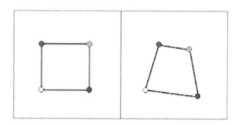

Figure 4-9. *Nonaffine transformation*

At the core of transformation is a matrix multiplication of the image. You will now look at different components of this matrix and the resulting image.

Translation

Image translation is about the displacement of images from the original position in any direction and within a frame of context. Figure 4-10 shows the transformation matrix.

$$T = \begin{bmatrix} 0 & 1 & t_x \\ 1 & 0 & ty \end{bmatrix}$$

Figure 4-10. *Transformation matrix*

Here, tx is translation in the *x* direction, and ty is in the *y* direction in an image reference. After choosing different values of the translation matrix, the resulting translation images will look like Figure 4-11.

Figure 4-11. *Resulting translation images*

The code for creating this translation is as follows; you can change the values of tx and ty to generate different translations:

```
1  import cv2
2  import numpy as np
3
4  iamge = cv2.imread('.images/pup.jpg')
5  num_rows, num_cols = iamge.shape[:2]
6
7  translation_matrix = np.float32([ [1,0,70], [0,1,110] ])
8  image_translation = cv2.warpAffine(iamge, translation_
   matrix, (num_cols, num_rows))
9  cv2.imshow('Translation', image_translation)
10 cv2.waitKey()
```

The `warpAffline()` function is used to define the translated image.

Rotation

Another form of image transformation is rotation. In this section, you will look at how to rotate the images in at a certain angle.

To understand this, let's see how to handle rotation mathematically. Rotation is also a form of transformation, and it can be achieved using the transformation matrix shown in Figure 4-12.

$$R = \begin{bmatrix} \cos\theta & -\sin\theta \\ \sin\theta & \cos\theta \end{bmatrix}$$

***Figure 4-12.** Transformation matrix*

Here, θ is the angle of rotation in the counterclockwise direction. OpenCV provides closer control over the creation of this matrix through the function `getRotationMatrix2D`. You can specify the point around which the image will be rotated, the angle of rotation in degrees, and a scaling factor for the image. Once you have the transformation matrix, you can use the same `warpAffine()` function to apply this matrix to any image.

The following code helps to expand the context to ensure the image is not cut off when it is rotated:

```
1  import cv2
2  import numpy as np
3
4  img = cv2.imread('images/pup.jpg')
5  num_rows, num_cols = img.shape[:2]
6
```

```
7   translation_matrix = np.float32([ [1,0,int(0.5*num_cols)],
    [0,1,int(0.5*num_rows)] ])
8   2*num_cols, 2*num_rows))
9   rotation_matrix = cv2.getRotationMatrix2D((num_cols, num_rows),
30, img_translation = cv2.warpAffine(img, translation_matrix, (1)
10  img_rotation = cv2.warpAffine(img_translation, rotation_
    matrix, (2*num_cols, 2*num_rows))
11
12  cv2.imshow('Rotation', img_rotation)
13  cv2.waitKey()
```

Figure 4-13 shows the output of this code.

Figure 4-13. *Output of rotation code*

Image Scaling

Image scaling is about resizing an image by changing its pixel dimensions. This is one of the most common operations in computer vision. Whenever you resize an image, there are multiple ways to fill in the pixel values. When you are enlarging an image, you need to fill up the pixel values in between the pixel locations. When you are shrinking an image, you need to take the best representative value. When you are scaling by a noninteger value, you need to interpolate values appropriately so that the quality of the image is maintained. There are multiple ways to do interpolation. If you are enlarging an image, it's preferable to use linear or cubic interpolation. If you are shrinking an image, it's preferable to use the area-based interpolation. Cubic interpolation is computationally more complex and hence slower than linear interpolation. But the quality of the resulting image will be higher.

OpenCV provides a function called `resize()` to achieve image scaling. The following OpenCV Python code helps to resize images:

```
1   import cv2
2   import numpy as np
3
4   img = cv2.imread('images/pup.jpg')
5
6   img_scaled = cv2.resize(img,None,fx=1.2, fy=1.2,
    interpolation = cv2.INTER_LINEAR)
7   cv2.imshow('Scaling - Linear Interpolation', img_scaled)
8   img_scaled = cv2.resize(img,None,fx=1.2, fy=1.2,
    interpolation = cv2.INTER_CUBIC)
9   cv2.imshow('Scaling - Cubic Interpolation', img_scaled)
10  img_scaled = cv2.resize(img,(450, 400), interpolation =
    cv2.INTER_AREA)
11  cv2.imshow('Scaling - Skewed Size', img_scaled) cv2.waitKey()
12
13  cv2.waitKey()
```

Figure 4-14 shows the sample outputs of rotating an image.

Figure 4-14. *Outputs of rotating an image*

Edge Detection

Edge detection has a lot of prominence in computer vision. It deals with the contours of an image usually denoted as an outline of a specific object in an image. Figure 4-15 shows an example of an output from an edge detection implementation.

Figure 4-15. *Edge detection implementation*

There are many edge detection algorithms such as Sobel, Laplacian, and Canny among others. The Canny edge detection algorithm is the most widely used for both ease of use and accuracy levels. The following OpenCV Python program is an example of implementing the Canny edge detection algorithm.

For more details about the Sobel, Laplacian, and Canny edge detection algorithms, refer to www.rroij.com/open-access/performance-analysis-of-canny-and-sobel-edgedetection-algorithms-in-image-mining.php?aid=43752.

```
1   import opencv
2   import numppy as np
3
4   image = cv2.imread('./images/dolphin.jpg')
5   hsv = cv2.cvtColor(frame, cv2.COLOR_BGR2HSV)
6
7   lower_red = np.array([30,150,50])
8   upper_red = np.array([255,255,180])
9
10  mask = cv2.inRange(hsv, lower_red, upper_red)
11  res = cv2.bitwise_and(frame,frame, mask= mask)
12
13  cv2.imshow('Original',frame)
14  edges = cv2.Canny(frame,100,200)
15  cv2.imshow('Edges',edges)
16
17  k = cv2.waitKey(5) & 0xFF
18  if k == 27:
19    break
20
21  cv2.destroyAllWindows()
22  cap.release()
```

Image Segmentation

As a quick recap, *pixels* on images store values. These values represent features of an image that give information about image statistics. These values group dark to light transitions to form borders, and the borders divide scenes into different objects. Borders connect to each other and reveal contours. Contours play an important role in many computer vision algorithms. They help to find objects, to separate one instance of something from another, and finally to understand the whole scene.

This section covers everything that deals with contours in OpenCV. You'll learn about methods for finding, using, and displaying contours, as well as consider basic segmentation methods.

Let's start drawing contours from a given image, as shown in Figure 4-16. The image has four different shapes.

Figure 4-16. *Image with four shapes*

The following is the step-by-step guide to building the implementation:

Step 1: Load the image.

```
import cv2
import numpy as np

# Load our image
image = cv2.imread('images/bunchofshapes.jpg')
```

Step 2: Convert the loaded image to grayscale.

```
# Grayscale our image
gray = cv2.cvtColor(image,cv2.COLOR_BGR2GRAY)
```

Step 3: Get the contours using the Canny edge detection function.

```
# Find Canny edges
edged = cv2.Canny(gray, 50, 200)
cv2.imshow('1 - Canny Edges', edged)
cv2.waitKey(0)
```

Step 4: Find the contours and print how many contours were found.

```
# Find contours and print how many were found
contours, hierarchy = cv2.findContours(edged.copy(), cv2.RETR_EXTERNAL, cv2.CHAIN_APPROX_NONE)
print ("Number of contours found = ", len(contours))
```

Step 5: Finally, draw the contours.

```
#Draw all contours
cv2.drawContours(blank_image, contours, -1, (0,255,0), 3)
cv2.imshow('2 - All Contours over blank image', blank_image)
cv2.waitKey(0)
```

Figure 4-17 shows the output of this program.

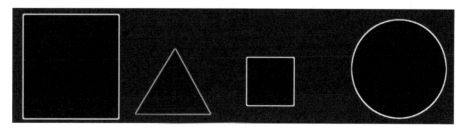

Figure 4-17. *Drawing contours*

Line Detection

In this section, you will learn how to detect lines given an image. You can use this technique for detecting lanes for self-driving cars or for drawing lines and grids on a chess board, for example. There are two different notations for lines in OpenCV: Hough lines and probabilistic Hough lines.

A straight line is usually represented as y = mx +c, and Hough lines are represented as $\rho = x \cos \theta + y \sin \theta$. Figure 4-18 shows an example of a chess board grid and the output where the lines are detected by an OpenCV Python program.

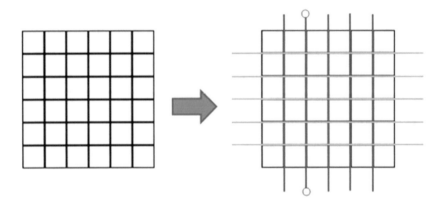

Figure 4-18. *Chess board grid*

The following is the step-by-step guide to building the implementation:

Step 1: Load the image, convert it to grayscale, and extract the contours.

```python
import cv2
import numpy as np

image = cv2.imread('images/chess.jpg')

# Grayscale and Canny Edges extracted
gray = cv2.cvtColor(image, cv2.COLOR_BGR2GRAY)
edges = cv2.Canny(gray, 100, 170, apertureSize = 3)
```

Step 2: Run Hough lines with the following parameters:

```
# Run HoughLines using a rho accuracy of 1 pixel
# theta accuracy of np.pi / 180 which is 1 degree
# Our line threshold is set to 240 (number of points on line)
lines = cv2.HoughLines(edges, 1, np.pi / 180, 240)
```

Step 3: Iterate through each identified line and highlight it on the image.

```
# We iterate through each line and convert it to the format
# required by cv.lines (i.e. requiring end points)
for rho, theta in lines[0]:
    a = np.cos(theta)
    b = np.sin(theta)
    x0 = a * rho
    y0 = b * rho
    x1 = int(x0 + 1000 * (-b))
    y1 = int(y0 + 1000 * (a))
    x2 = int(x0 - 1000 * (-b))
    y2 = int(y0 - 1000 * (a))
    cv2.line(image, (x1, y1), (x2, y2), (255, 0, 0), 2)
```

Step 4: Finally, show the image that has the lines highlighted.

```
cv2.imshow('Hough Lines', image)
cv2.waitKey(0)
cv2.destroyAllWindows()
```

Circle Detection

Similar to the previous line detection implementation, let's now look at circle detection. In lieu of Hough lines, you will use Hough circles.

Load an image like Figure 4-19 for circle detection.

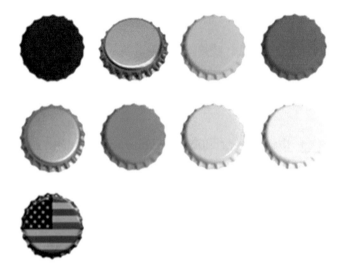

Figure 4-19. *Circle detection*

The following is the OpenCV Python code that loads the image in Figure 4-19, converts it to grayscale, identifies the contours, extracts the Hough circles, and then draws them:

```
1  import cv2
2  import numpy as np
3  import cv2.cv as cv
4
5  image = cv2.imread('images/bottlecaps.jpg')
6  gray = cv2.cvtColor(image, cv2.COLOR_BGR2GRAY)
7
8  blur = cv2.medianBlur(gray, 5)
9
10  circles = cv2.HoughCircles(blur, cv.CV_HOUGH_GRADIENT, 1.5, 10)
11  #circles = cv2.HoughCircles(gray, cv.CV_HOUGH_GRADIENT, 1, 10)
12
```

```
13  circles = np.uint16(np.around(circles))
14
15  for i in circles[0,:]:
16      # draw the outer circle
17      cv2.circle(image,(i[0], i[1]), i[2], (255, 0, 0), 2)
18
19      # draw the center of the circle
20      cv2.circle(image, (i[0], i[1]), 2, (0, 255, 0), 5)
21
22  cv2.imshow('detected circles', image)
23  cv2.waitKey(0)
24  cv2.destroyAllWindows()
```

Figure 4-20 shows the output of this program.

Figure 4-20. *Output of circle detection*

Conclusion

In this chapter, you learned how to do image processing, which includes image manipulations such as drawing on images, changing pixels, transforming images, performing edge detection, blurring, and others. Similarly to image segmentation, you learned how to detect the contours of an object and highlight them.

The next chapter will cover object detection use cases and provide a step-by-step guide for implementing them using built-in OpenCV Python functions.

CHAPTER 5

Object Detection and Recognition

In the previous chapter, you learned about image segmentation and contours. You also learned how to detect lines and circles using Hough lines and circles in OpenCV. In this chapter, you will learn how to detect objects and label them. Object detection is one of the most widely used capabilities of computer vision in multiple domains. In Chapter 1, you saw some real-world use cases. In this chapter, you will start with object detection and then move on to object recognition, landmark identification, and finally handwriting recognition.

The following topics are covered in this chapter:

- Introduction to object detection and its uses

- How objects are stored and the different ways of extracting features such as SIFT, SURF, FAST, BRIEF, and so on

- Handwriting recognition

Basics of Object Detection

Detecting objects in an image is a crucial capability of a computer vision application. Object detection/recognition is used in labeling scenes, robotic navigation, self-driving cars, face and body part recognition, disease and cancer detection, objects in satellite images, handwriting recognition, and many more.

© Sunila Gollapudi 2019
S. Gollapudi, *Learn Computer Vision Using OpenCV*,
https://doi.org/10.1007/978-1-4842-4261-2_5

Figure 5-1 shows an example of real-time object detection and labeling done for a given image.

Figure 5-1. *Real-time object detection and labeling*

Object Detection vs. Object Recognition

In Figure 5-1, we only marked or detected if there was a truck or a dog. We did not recognize any specific qualities such as the model or color of the car or the color or breed of the dog because the objective was to just identify what objects are in the image. *Object recognition* is the method of identifying an object within an image. In the case of object recognition, you first detect the car, and on the cropped car you apply recognizers to recognize the features of the car. This is similar with faces as well.

While humans can identify a variety of objects effortlessly, for computers it is a complex problem to solve with accuracy. It has eluded computer vision researchers for decades now and has become the holy grail of computer vision.

Depending on the position and angle of the object, the object detection task is difficult. Defining a bounding box for each object is important.

Template Matching

As part of object detection and recognition, you need to do shape analysis and feature analysis. To do this, there is a robust technique called *template matching*. This technically is a brute-force algorithm or a simple mechanism to extract an object based on a previously acquired template.

OpenCV has a `matchTemplate()` function to perform template matching.

This function takes a "sliding window" of the image being queried and slides it across the image it is searching for to determine its presence. It does this one pixel at a time. Then, for each of these locations, a correlation coefficient is calculated if there is a match at all. Regions with a high correlation are the regions that match.

Figure 5-2 shows a typical object detection using matching. This method uses a template to detect an object after segmentation. If the segmented object is similar to the template, then the object detection process is concluded; otherwise, another template is picked for a similarity check.

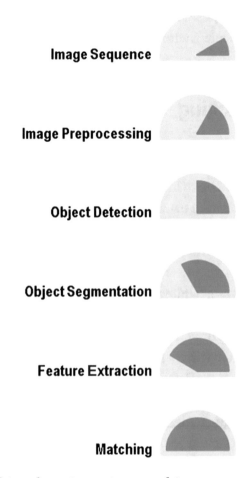

Figure 5-2. *Object detection using matching*

The following is the example code for template matching in OpenCV using the matchTemplate() function:

```
1  import cv2
2  import numpy as np
3
4  # Load input image and convert to grayscale
5  image = cv2.imread('./images/inputImage.jpg')
```

```
 6  cv2.imshow('Where is this image?', image)
 7  cv2.waitKey(0)
 8  gray = cv2.cvtColor(image, cv2.COLOR_BGR2GRAY)
 9
10  # Load Bigger image
11  bigger_image = cv2.imread('./images/searchImage.jpg',0)
12
13  result = cv2.matchTemplate(gray, template, cv2.TM_CCOEFF)
14  min_val, max_val, min_loc, max_loc = cv2.minMaxLoc(result)
15
16  #Create Bounding Box
17  top_left = max_loc
18  bottom_right = (top_left[0] + 50, top_left[1] + 50)
19  cv2.rectangle(image, top_left, bottom_right, (0,0,255), 5)
20
21  cv2.imshow('Where is input image?', image)
22  cv2.waitKey(0)
23  cv2.destroyAllWindows()
```

The input image is searched in the bigger image. Use the matchTemplate() function by passing the grayscale image.

Lines 1 and 2: Import the OpenCV and NumPy libraries.

Lines 4 through 8: Load the image that needs to be searched for and convert it to grayscale.

Line 10: Loads the bigger image in which the input image needs to be searched for.

Lines 13 and 14: cv2.matchTemplate() returns a correlation map, essentially a grayscale image. This image has each pixel that denotes the extent to which its neighborhood matches with the template. The minMaxLoc function returns the max and min intensity values as an array that includes the location of these intensities.

MaxVal is the location with the highest intensity in the image. This is returned by matchTemplate() and corresponds to the best matching input image with regard to the defined template.

Lines 16 through 19: Draw a boundary with a padding value of 50 and a thickness value of 5 pixels and in blue around the contours of the matching image.

Challenges with Template Matching

While template matching helps when doing object detection and recognition in an image, there are several challenges with this methodology. If the image is rotated, scaled, modified for colors or brightness, or transformed, it is difficult to match or detect an input object in the image.

Understanding Image "Features"

With the challenges of the template matching approach, you will now learn about image feature–driven object detection and recognition. To start, let's look at what features are in the context of image processing.

Features correspond to the properties or attributes of an image. They play an important role in building accurate computer vision applications. Pixels, as you learned in Chapter 1, are used to compare two images.

The most basic form of feature detection is point features. In applications such as panorama creation on our smartphones, each image is stitched with the corresponding previous image. This stitching requires the correct orientation of an image overlapped with pixel-level accuracy. Computing corresponding pixels between two images requires pixel matching.

Interesting and Uninteresting Points

Within an image there can be interesting and uninteresting points. Interesting points in an image are those that can give the most information about the object in the image, and uninteresting points give either zero or no information about the image or the object in the image. Figure 5-3 shows an image of the Eiffel Tower with the image feature points and what could be an interesting or uninteresting point. The sky could be an uninteresting feature because it hardly gives the context of the monument. A point on the Eiffel Tower does give more information about it and hence becomes an interesting feature.

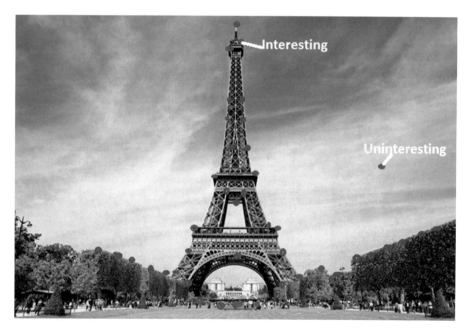

Figure 5-3. *Image feature points*

The following are some characteristics of an interesting, or good, feature:

- **Is repeatable**: The same feature can be found in several other images despite any image transformations.

- **Is salient/distinctive/unique:** The feature is unique and has a distinctive description in the use case context.

- **Is compact in number:** There are a measurable number of pixels that describe the object in context.

- **Is local**: The object in context occupies a relatively smaller area within an image.

Types of Image Features

There are primarily three types of image features: edges, regions, and corner features. These features of objects are used to track objects in an image by observing the change in intensity, as shown in Figure 5-4.

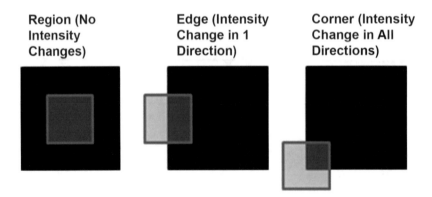

Figure 5-4. *Changes in intensity*

Feature Matching

Feature matching can be done in one of the following cases:

- There are two images, and you want to quantify whether these images match each other. There will usually be a comparison metric that is applied.

- There is a large database of images, and for every new image, you need to perform matching against the database of images. A smaller search criterion is stored and then compared with the input image instead of recomputing everything for every image in the database. This is called a *feature vector* of the image. For every new input image, a similar vector is extracted and stored.

- As an alternative approach, you have a small portion of the image stored as a template. The goal is to check whether an image has this template. This will require matching key points from the template against the given sample image. If the match value is greater than a threshold, you can say the sample image has a region similar to the given template. There is a possibility of showing where in the sample image your template image is.

Image Corners As Features

In this section, you will learn how to use corners as features for object detection and recognition. While corners do not necessarily provide all the details of the objects, they are helpful in many cases. As indicated in Figure 5-4, when the blue frame is moved around the image and in particular you see that there is an intensity change in all directions (Figure 5-4, section 3), then that is identified as the corner of the image.

Let's look at some OpenCV code that explains how to identify a corner. You will use an algorithm in the OpenCV library called the Harris corner algorithm.

Harris Corner Algorithm

This algorithm helps identify the inside corner of an image by checking the area that has maximum variations in intensity.

In 1988 Chris Harris and Mike Stephens developed this algorithm that can perform both edge detection and corner detection. Hence, this algorithm was named after one of the authors.

In OpenCV, the `cv2.cornerHarris()` function is used to achieve the corner detection.

```
cv2.cornerHarris(image, blockSize, ksize, k)
```

This function takes four arguments.

- img is the image to be analyzed; it must be in grayscale and with float32 values.

- blockSize is the size of the window considered for the corner detection.

- ksize is a parameter for the derivative of Sobel.

- k is a free parameter for the Harris equation.

The following OpenCV code takes an image input, identifies the corners, and marks them:

```
1  import cv2
2  import numpy as np
3  from matplotlib import pyplot as plt
4
5  img = cv2.imread('blackandwhite.jpg',0)
6  img = np.float32(img)
```

```
7  corners = cv2.cornerHarris(img,2,3,0.04)
8
9  corners = cv2.cornerHarris(img,2,3,0.04)
10
11 plt.subplot(2,1,1), plt.imshow(corners ,cmap = 'jet')
12 plt.title('Harris Corner Detection'), plt.xticks([]),
   plt.yticks([])
13
14 img2 = cv2.imread('blackandwhite.jpg')
15 corners2 = cv2.dilate(corners, None, iterations=3)
16 img2[corners2>0.01*corners2.max()] = [255,0,0]
17
18 plt.subplot(2,1,2),plt.imshow(img2,cmap = 'gray')
19 plt.title('Canny Edge Detection'), plt.xticks([]),
   plt.yticks([])
20
21 plt.show()
```

In the previous code, line 7 is the place where the Harris corner algorithm is invoked. Once the corners are identified, they are highlighted using the dilate() function, and the identified pixels are assigned the color red for showing in a new window. Figure 5-5 shows the input and output images.

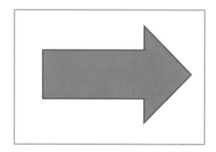 

Figure 5-5. *Input and output images, corner detection*

Figure 5-6 shows another example of an input and output of corner detection.

Figure 5-6. *Another example of corner detection*

However, there are several challenges when corners are used as features for object detection. While corner matching works well with image rotations, translations or any photometric changes such as brightness, intensity changes, and image scaling does not work.

Feature Tracking and Matching Flow

In this section, you will learn the standard flow for feature extraction and matching. Figure 5-7 shows the generic steps involved in feature extraction.

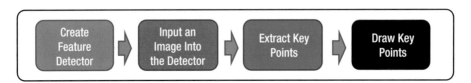

Figure 5-7. *Feature extraction workflow*

The first step is to create a standard feature extractor and then extract robust features from a given image. This process involves scanning through the whole image for possible features and then thresholding them. There are several techniques for selecting features such as SIFT, SURF, FAST, BRIEF, ORB detectors, and so on. In the next sections, we will cover these methods in depth. The feature extracted, in some cases, needs to be converted into a more descriptive form so that it can be learned by the model or can be stored for re-reading.

In the case of feature matching, say you are given a sample image and want to see whether this matches a reference image. After feature detection and extraction, as shown previously, a distance metric is formed to compute the distance between features of the sample with respect to the features of reference. If this distance is less than the threshold, you can say the two images are similar.

Scale Variant Feature Transform

Scale Variant Feature Transform (SIFT) is currently patented but can be freely used for academic purposes.

You saw in the previous section some of the challenges with using corners for feature extraction and how it doesn't work well when scaling up. In Figure 5-8, you can see how detecting a corner can fail.

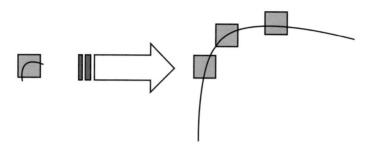

Figure 5-8. *Corner detection failure*

The SIFT approach addresses this challenge. You can find more details about SIFT and how it works at `www.inf.fu-berlin.de/lehre/SS09/CV/uebungen/uebung09/SIFT.pdf`.

OpenCV has built-in functions for SIFT, but they need to be explicitly installed since they are patented.

The following steps and code show how to implement the SIFT functions:

1. Load an image and convert it to grayscale.

2. Construct a SIFT object using the `SIFT()` function.

3. The `sift.detect()` function finds the keypoint in the images. You can pass a mask if you want to search only part of the image. Each keypoint is a special structure that has many attributes such as its (x,y) coordinates, size of the meaningful neighborhood, angle that specifies its orientation, response that specifies the strength of the keypoints, and so on.

4. OpenCV also provides the `cv2.drawKeyPoints()` function, which draws small circles on the locations of the keypoints. If you pass the flag `cv2.DRAW_MATCHES_FLAGS_DRAW_RICH_KEYPOINTS` to it, it will draw a circle with the size of the keypoint, and it will even show its orientation.

```
1  import cv2
2  import numpy as np
3
4  image = cv2.imread('images/input.jpg')
5  gray = cv2.cvtColor(image, cv2.COLOR_BGR2GRAY)
6
```

```
 7   #Create SIFT Feature Detector object
 8   sift = cv2.SIFT()
 9
10   #Detect key points
11   keypoints = sift.detect(gray, None)
12   print("Number of keypoints Detected: ", len(keypoints))
13
14   # Draw rich key points on input image
15   image = cv2.drawKeypoints(image, keypoints,
     flags=cv2.DRAW_MATCHES_FLAGS_DRAW_RICH_KEYPOINTS)
16
17   cv2.imshow('Feature Method - SIFT', image)
18   cv2.waitKey(0)
19   cv2.destroyAllWindows()
```

The program results are shown in Figure 5-9; the input image is shown on top, and the output image is shown at the bottom.

Figure 5-9. *SIFT example (source: AIShack)*

Speeded-Up Robust Features

Like SIFT, Speeded-Up Robust Features (SURF) is patented but can be
openly used for academic purposes. It needs to be explicitly imported
since it is patented. You can find more details on what SURF is and how it
works at `www.vision.ee.ethz.ch/~surf/eccv06.pdf`.

OpenCV provides functions for SURF like SIFT. Similar to SIFT, SURF
has functions such as `detect()` and `compute()`. The following code sample
shows the implementation steps:

```
1  import cv2
2  import numpy as np
```

```
 3
 4   image = cv2.imread('images/input.jpg')
 5   gray = cv2.cvtColor(image, cv2.COLOR_BGR2GRAY)
 6
 7   #Create SURF Feature Detector object
 8   surf = cv2.SURF()
 9
10   # Only features, whose hessian is larger than hessianThreshold
are  retained by the detector
11   surf.hessianThreshold = 500
12   keypoints, descriptors = surf.detectAndCompute(gray, None)
13   print "Number of keypoints Detected: ", len(keypoints)
14
15   # Draw rich key points on input image
16   image = cv2.drawKeypoints(image, keypoints,
     flags=cv2.DRAW_MATCHES_FLAGS_DRAW_RICH_KEYPOINTS)
17
18   cv2.imshow('Feature Method - SURF', image)
19   cv2.waitKey()
20   cv2.destroyAllWindows()
```

Features from Accelerated Segment Test

Features from Accelerated Segment Test (FAST) was first introduced in 2006 by Edward Rosten and Tom Drummond. The previous feature detectors are not useful for real-time applications, for example those with video cameras collecting real-time images or robots. These use cases will fail if any delay is caused in feature detection at runtime. The FAST algorithm uses a pixel neighborhood to compute key points in an image.

For the neighborhood, three flags are defined: cv2.FAST_FEATURE_
DETECTOR_TYPE_5_8, cv2.FAST_FEATURE_DETECTOR_TYPE_7_12, and cv2.
FAST_FEATURE_DETECTOR_TYPE_9_16. The following is some simple code to
detect and draw the FAST feature points:

```
1   import cv2
2   import numpy as np
3
4   image = cv2.imread('images/input.jpg')
5   gray = cv2.cvtColor(image, cv2.COLOR_BGR2GRAY)
6
7   # Create FAST Detector object
8   fast = cv2.FastFeatureDetector()
9
10  # Obtain Key points, by default non max suppression is On
11  # to turn off set fast.setBool('nonmaxSuppression', False)
12  keypoints = fast.detect(gray, None)
13  print "Number of keypoints Detected: ", len(keypoints)
14
15  # Draw rich keypoints on input image
16  image = cv2.drawKeypoints(image, keypoints,
    flags=cv2.DRAW_MATCHES_FLAGS_DRAW_RICH_KEYPOINTS)
17
18  cv2.imshow('Feature Method - FAST', image)
19  cv2.waitKey()
20  cv2.destroyAllWindows()
```

Binary Robust Independent Elementary Features

Binary Robust Independent Elementary Features (BRIEF) is a relatively
faster method feature descriptor calculator and matching algorithm.
Additionally, it provides a higher-recognition rate except for the cases

where there is plane rotation. You can find more details about what BRIEF is and how it works at `http://cvlabwww.epfl.ch/~lepetit/papers/calonder_pami11.pdf`.

The following code shows the computation of BRIEF descriptors with the help of a CenSurE detector:

```
1   import cv2
2   import numpy as np
3
4   image = cv2.imread('images/input.jpg')
5   gray = cv2.cvtColor(image, cv2.COLOR_BGR2GRAY)
6
7   # Create FAST detector object
8   fast = cv2.FastFeatureDetector()
9
10  # Create BRIEF extractor object
11  brief = cv2.DescriptorExtractor_create("BRIEF")
12
13  # Determine key points
14  keypoints = fast.detect(gray, None)
15
16  # Obtain descriptors and new final keypoints using BRIEF
17  keypoints, descriptors = brief.compute(gray, keypoints)
18  print "Number of keypoints Detected: ", len(keypoints)
19
20  # Draw rich keypoints on input image
21  image = cv2.drawKeypoints(image, keypoints, flags=cv2.DRAW_
    MATCHES_FLAGS_DRAW_RICH_KEYPOINTS)
22
23  cv2.imshow('Feature Method - BRIEF', image)
24  cv2.waitKey()
25  cv2.destroyAllWindows()
```

Oriented FAST and Rotated BRIEF

ORB is a combination of a FAST keypoint detector and a BRIEF descriptor with additional performance fixes. This method applies the FAST technique to identify the keypoints followed by the measurement of the top *n* points using the Harris corner method.

OpenCV has an ORB() function that can use a feature2d common interface. For more details on what ORB is and how it works, refer to http://www.willowgarage.com/sites/default/files/orb_final.pdf.

```
1   import numpy as np
2   import cv2
3   from matplotlib import pyplot as plt
4
5   img = cv2.imread('simple.jpg',0)
6
7   # Initiate STAR detector
8   orb = cv2.ORB()
9
10  # find the keypoints with ORB
11  kp = orb.detect(img,None)
12
13  # compute the descriptors with ORB
14  kp, des = orb.compute(img, kp)
15
16  # draw only keypoints location,not size and orientation
17  img2 = cv2.drawKeypoints(img,kp,color=(0,255,0), flags=0)
18  plt.imshow(img2),plt.show()
```

Conclusion

In this chapter, you learned about the difference between object detection and recognition. You learned about what image features are and how they are important for object detection and feature tracking. You also learned how to detect corners, especially using OpenCV's built-in functions. Additionally, the chapter covered important detectors such as SIFT, SURF, FAST, BRIEF, and ORB with steps for implementing them using the OpenCV and Python libraries.

In the next chapter, you will learn how to do object tracking in motion using specific OpenCV functions.

CHAPTER 6

Motion Analysis and Object Tracking

The goal of this chapter is to cover motion analysis and the tracking of objects. You will learn how to get information about different types of objects in motion, understand techniques to remove background and foreground information, and see real-time tracking options with hands-on implementation steps. The topics in this chapter are an extension of the object detection and recognition techniques you learned about in Chapter 5 and hence require a thorough understanding of that chapter.

The following topics are covered in detail in this chapter:

- Object tracking techniques, including using frame differencing to learn some information about an object in motion

- Background and foreground subtraction

- Using optical flow techniques for object feature tracking

- Building interactive object tracking using the meanshift and camshift techniques

© Sunila Gollapudi 2019
S. Gollapudi, *Learn Computer Vision Using OpenCV*,
https://doi.org/10.1007/978-1-4842-4261-2_6

Introduction to Object Tracking

Object tracking is the process of estimating the exact position of an object while the object is in motion or across consecutive image frames within a video. In simple terms, it is all about tracking an object across a sequence of images or measuring its relative movement with respect to other objects in the frame. Object detection, covered in Chapter 5, forms an important step in object tracking. Figure 6-1 shows the basic steps for tracking an object.

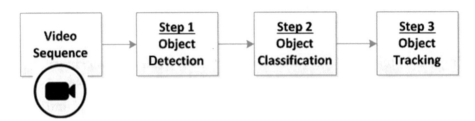

Figure 6-1. *Basic object tracking*

There are many applications of object tracking, such as security surveillance, augmented reality, traffic monitoring, self-driving cars, action recognition, and so on. In the case of augmented reality, within the context of a video, a three-dimensional object is placed based on the relative disposition of the other objects in the video, thus giving an impression of its real existence in that location. In the case of self-driving cars, the distances of the car in motion to the other vehicles moving alongside it are measured to compute the exact speed at which the self-driving car needs to go. If the distance relative to a neighboring car increases, this means the current speed can be increased, and vice versa. The increased speed should not cross the speed limit restrictions defined for that area. In effect, this process can turn out to be complex because of the large number of parameters influencing the decision-making process.

The ability to track an object in a video depends on multiple factors, such as knowledge about what the object in context is, what parameters of the object are being tracked, and what type of video is showing the object.

Challenges of Object Tracking

In addition to all the challenges that apply to image processing (covered in Chapter 1) that in general also apply to object tracking, the following challenges need to be dealt with:

- **Object occlusion**: When the target image is hidden behind something, it is difficult to both detect and update when future images come in.

- **Speed**: When the motion of an object is fast, the output video usually is blurred or jittery. Hence, any sudden changes in the motion of cameras lead to problems in tracking applications.

- **Shape**: Tracking objects that are nonrigid (i.e. the shape is not constant) will result in failure on object detection and thus tracking.

- **False positives**: When there are multiple similar objects, it is hard to match which object is targeted in subsequent images. The tracker may lose the current object in terms of detection and start tracking a similar object.

These challenges can make applications crash suddenly or give a completely incorrect estimate of an object's location.

Object Detection Techniques for Tracking

Object tracking uses object detection techniques that are applied across consecutive frames of a video. As you learned in Chapter 5, object detection is about defining a bounding box for an object. Since a video has a set of consecutive image frames, the bounding box application will need to be extended and applied for every frame. For object tracking to show the required results, the object that is being tracked is assumed to be available across all the frames. A robust matching formula can confirm that the same object is between two frames.

The first step in the process of object tracking is to identify objects of interest in the video sequence and to cluster pixels of these objects. Since moving objects are typically the primary source of information, most methods focus on the detection of such objects. This is also referred to as *tracking by detection*. Figure 6-2 shows the object detection techniques applied for object tracking.

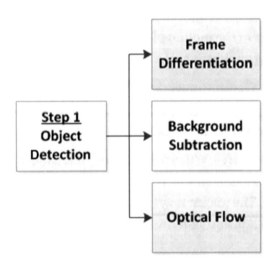

Figure 6-2. *Object detection techniques*

Frame Differentiation

Frame differencing is a technique to measure the difference between two video frames by observing the position of one or more objects in context. The pixel definitions are observed for any changes as this is an indication of changes in the image. A pixel change indicates a change in the image.

Frame differentiation is all about determining the presence of moving objects by calculating the pixel difference between two consecutive images in a video. While the general calculation is simple and easy to implement, complexity creeps in because of the "moving" object, which can jeopardize the accuracy. To differentiate the real movement from noise, some blur, and threshold techniques as the difference in the frame could come from a change in the light conditions as well. Frame differentiation techniques have high accuracy and relatively lower or moderate computational time; this method works well for static backgrounds.

Background Subtraction

Background subtraction is an important preprocessing technique in vision-based applications because it helps separate the background from the foreground in video streams. An interesting use case for this technique is a ticket counter where the background is static but the foreground has visitors coming to the counter to buy tickets. The requirement could be counting the number of visitors coming to the counter in the day. In this case, you first need to extract each person alone.

If there is an image or a frame of video that just has the static background and no moving visitors, it is a straightforward task because all you need to do is subtract the new image from the background to extract the foreground alone. The real-world cases wouldn't be this simple, so extracting the background is a mandatory step. Newer complexities would arise when there is a shadow, since as the shadow moves, a part of the background would be removed too; therefore, the accuracy of the solution suffers. All background subtraction methods are moderate on accuracy as well as computational time. The Gaussian mixture method requires less memory but cannot cope with a multimodal background. The approximate median method requires a buffer with the recent pixel values. There are three categories of algorithms built for this purpose in OpenCV 3.*x*. The functions `createBackgroundSubtractorMOG()`, `createBackgroundSubtractorMOG2()`, and `createBackgroundSubtractorGMG()` have been replaced by much

more efficient KNN-based background subtraction algorithms. The MOG()
and MOG2() functions are Gaussian mixture-based methods that use
background and foreground segmentation analysis. These functions are
available only up to OpenCV 2.1.*x.*

The GMG() function adopts Bayesians methods for background and
foreground segmentation. Similar to MOG() functions, the GMG() function is
not available beyond OpenCV 2.1.*x.*

The function createBackgroundSubtractorKNN() in OpenCV iterates
through each frame of the video and morphs the foreground with the
background, thus helping the focus to be just on the object that needs to be
tracked across frames.

The K-nearest neighbor (KNN) algorithm classifies unknown data
points by finding the *most common class* among the "k" closest examples.
Each data point in the *k* closest examples adds to the weight, and the
one maximum weightage is used to classify the object. This algorithm is
synonymous to the English saying, "Tell me who your neighbors are, and
I'll tell you who you are."

For more details on how the algorithm works and its syntax, please
refer to https://docs.opencv.org/3.4/db/d5c/tutorial_py_bg_
subtraction.html.

The following code sample demonstrates how to implement the KNN
method for background subtraction:

```
1  import numpy as np
2  import cv2
3
4  cap = cv2.VideoCapture(0)
5
6  kernel = cv2.getStructuringElement(cv2.MORPH_ELLIPSE,(3,3))
7  fgbg = cv2.createBackgroundSubtractorKNN()
8
9  while(1):
```

```
10       ret, frame = cap.read()
11
12       fgmask = fgbg.apply(frame)
13       fgmask = cv2.morphologyEx(fgmask, cv2.MORPH_OPEN, kernel)
14
15       cv2.imshow('frame',fgmask)
16
17       if cv2.waitKey(1) == 13:
18           break
19
20   cap.release()
21   cv2.destroyAllWindows()
```

Figure 6-3 shows the output from this function.

Figure 6-3. *The output for implementing the KNN method*

Optical Flow

Optical flow denotes the motion of the objects in an image from one frame to another that is caused by either the motion of the image or the camera. It is represented as a 2D vector field that has each element representing the movement of the points from one frame to another. Figure 6-4 represents the movement of a ball from one position to another across five consecutive frames.

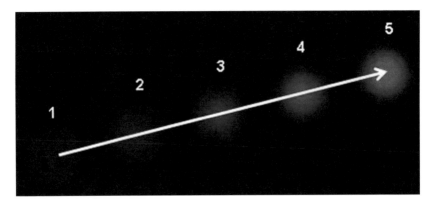

Figure 6-4. *Optical flow (source: OpenCV documentation)*

Some of the use cases of optical flow include representing the structure from motion, video compression, and video stabilization, among others. The optical flow method assumes that there is no change in the pixel intensities of an object between consecutive frames, and neighboring pixels also have similar motion. Optical flow methods are relatively high in computational time and moderate on accuracy.

Lucas–Kanade Differential Algorithm

The Lucas–Kanade differential algorithm helps in tracking the keypoints of an object in a video that has corner features such as tracking a car on the race track (by a drone).

OpenCV provides the `cv2.calcOpticalFlowPyrLK()` function for the Lucas–Kanade algorithm. First, consider the input video, which sets the parameters for corner detection and the Lucas–Kanade algorithm. Initialize a set of colors to create the trails of the object movement.

```
4  # Load video stream
5  cap = cv2.VideoCapture('images/test.avi')
6
7  # Set parameters for ShiTomasi corner detection
```

```
8   feature_params = dict( maxCorners = 100,
9                          qualityLevel = 0.3,
10                         minDistance = 7,
11                         blockSize = 7 )
12
13  # Set parameters for lucas kanade optical flow
14  lucas_kanade_params = dict( winSize  = (15,15),
15                      maxLevel = 2,
16                      criteria = (cv2.TERM_CRITERIA_EPS | cv2.
                        TERM_CRITERIA_COUNT, 10, 0.03))
```

Take the first frame, find the corners, and create a mask to track the movement in the next frames. Loop through each frame, calculate the optical flow, identify and store the good points, draw the track, and show the optical flow.

```
22  # Take first frame and find corners in it
23  ret, prev_frame = cap.read()
24  prev_gray = cv2.cvtColor(prev_frame, cv2.COLOR_BGR2GRAY)
25
26  # Find inital corner locations
27  prev_corners = cv2.goodFeaturesToTrack(prev_gray, mask =
    None, **feature_params)
28
29  # Create a mask image for drawing purposes
30  mask = np.zeros_like(prev_frame)
31
32  while(1):
33      ret, frame = cap.read()
34      frame_gray = cv2.cvtColor(frame, cv2.COLOR_BGR2GRAY)
35
36      # calculate optical flow
```

```
37      new_corners, status, errors = cv2.calcOpticalFlowPyrLK
                                          (prev_gray,
38                                        frame_gray,
39                                        prev_corners,
40                                        None,
41   **lucas_kanade_params)
42
43      # Select and store good points
44      good_new = new_corners[status==1]
45      good_old = prev_corners[status==1]
46
47      # Draw the tracks
48      for i,(new,old) in enumerate(zip(good_new, good_old)):
49          a, b = new.ravel()
50          c, d = old.ravel()
51          mask = cv2.line(mask, (a,b),(c,d), color[i].tolist(), 2)
52          frame = cv2.circle(frame, (a,b), 5, color[i].tolist(),-1)
53
54      img = cv2.add(frame,mask)
55
56      # Show Optical Flow
57      cv2.imshow('Optical Flow - Lucas-Kanade',img)
58      if cv2.waitKey(1) == 13: #13 is the Enter Key
59          break
60
61      # Now update the previous frame and previous points
62      prev_gray = frame_gray.copy()
63      prev_corners = good_new.reshape(-1,1,2)
```

Figure 6-5 shows the output of this program.

Figure 6-5. *The results of the Lucas–Kanade algorithm*

Dense Optical Flow Algorithm

Unlike the Lucas–Kanade method that looks at corner-like features, the dense optical flow algorithm looks at all the points on an image. Colors are used to reflect movement, with the hue representing the direction and the value representing the speed. This makes this algorithm relatively slower.

First, load the input video and get the hue colors for the first frame. For each frame, convert it to grayscale, compute the optical flow, and calculate the magnitude and the color to reflect the speed of the angle, mark the color in the frame, and show the video until the frames are exhausted.

```
4   # Load video stream
5   cap = cv2.VideoCapture("images/walking.avi")
6
7   # Get first frame
8   ret, first_frame = cap.read()
9   previous_gray = cv2.cvtColor(first_frame, cv2.COLOR_BGR2GRAY)
10  hsv = np.zeros_like(first_frame)
```

```
11  hsv[...,1] = 255
12
13  while True:
14
15      # Read of video file
16      ret, frame2 = cap.read()
17      next = cv2.cvtColor(frame2,cv2.COLOR_BGR2GRAY)
18
19      # Computes the dense optical flow using the Gunnar
        Farneback's algorithm
20      flow = cv2.calcOpticalFlowFarneback(previous_gray, next,
21                                    None, 0.5, 3, 15, 3,
                                      5, 1.2, 0)
22
23      # use flow to calculate the magnitude (speed) and angle
        of motion
24      # use these values to calculate the color to reflect
        speed and angle
25      magnitude, angle = cv2.cartToPolar(flow[...,0], flow[...,1])
26      hsv[...,0] = angle * (180 / (np.pi/2))
27      hsv[...,2] = cv2.normalize(magnitude, None, 0, 255,
        cv2.NORM_MINMAX)
28      final = cv2.cvtColor(hsv, cv2.COLOR_HSV2BGR)
29
30      # Show our demo of Dense Optical Flow
31      cv2.imshow('Dense Optical Flow', final)
32      if cv2.waitKey(1) == 13: #13 is the Enter Key
33          break
34
35      # Store current image as previous image
36      previous_gray = next
```

Figure 6-6 shows the output of this program.

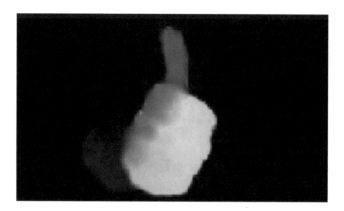

Figure 6-6. *The dense optical flow results*

Object Classification

Some objects extracted from the moving region could be birds, moving clouds, humans, or even swaying trees. We covered the shape features in Chapter 5 that apply for both stationary and moving objects. Figure 6-7 shows some standard approaches to classifying objects.

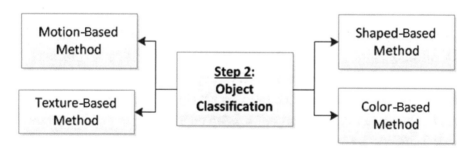

Figure 6-7. *Object classification techniques*

Shaped-Based Classification

There are many descriptions of shape information about motion regions such as the representation of points, blobs, or boxes to classify a given object. Classification is done on every frame for the object, and the results are stored in a histogram. Shape-based classification has a lower computational time and a relatively lower accuracy because template matching techniques can be applied.

Motion-Based Classification

Moving objects have a periodic property called *residual flow* that can be used for classification. Residual flow is used to analyze the rigidity and periodicity of the moving objects. Rigid objects present a little residual flow, whereas a nonrigid moving object like a human being has a higher average residual flow and displays a periodic component. Motion-based classification has a high computational time and relatively lower accuracy. Though it doesn't require templates, it fails to identify a static human/ nonrigid object.

Color-Based Classification

Color usually is not the most appropriate feature of an object to use for classification, but, among all the object features, color is fairly constant and can also be easily acquired. Furthermore, it is one of the features that can be exploited when needed. Color histograms are used to detect and track vehicles in real time. A Gaussian distribution model is used to understand the color distribution in a sequence of images, which is useful to segment the background and the object. Color-based classification has a higher computational time and relatively higher accuracy because template matching techniques can be applied.

Texture-Based Classification

This techniques uses gradient orientation in the selected portions of the image. This method can result in more accuracy because it uses overlapping contrast normalization in a dense grid of uniformly spaced calls. Texture-based classification has a higher computational time and relatively higher accuracy than other methods.

Object Tracking Methods

You learned about the basic definition and purpose of object tracking at the beginning of this chapter. As a quick recap, an object is tracked to extract objects, recognize and track objects, and make decisions about activities. Object tracking, at a high level, can be classified as point tracking, kernel-based tracking, and silhouette-based tracking (Figure 6-8).

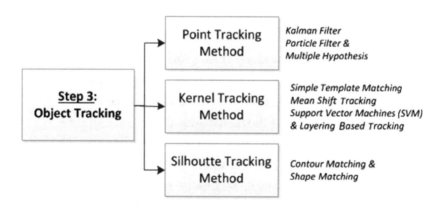

Figure 6-8. *Some object tracking techniques*

Both kernel- and silhouette-based tracking require the object to first appear in the scene, while point tracking works on object detection in every frame.

Point Tracking Method

Point tracking is done using the feature points of the moving object. There are three methods for point tracking: Kalman filtering, particle filtering, and multiple hypothesis.

- **Kalman filtering** uses a restrictive probability density propagation algorithm. It supports estimation of past, present, and future states using its efficient recursive estimation techniques. There are two kinds of equations: time update equations and measurement update equations. Time update equations provide a future state using the details of the current state and error covariance estimations, and measurement update equations help in the feedback process in the recursive flow. Kalman filtering assumes normal distribution of all variables, which results in poor approximation of future states of the variables.

- **Particle filtering** considers a variable at one time and generates all the models for that variable. This method supports the dynamicity of variable states and also allows for a new operation of resampling. Particle filtering overcomes the restrictions that Kalman filters pose because they use contours, color features, or texture mapping. This method uses Bayesian sequential importance. The sample technique recursively approaches the distribution using a finite set of weighted trials.

- **Multiple hypothesis tracking (MHT)** observes more than one frame for better tracking results. MHT is an iterative mechanism as well. Every iteration starts with an existing track and a hypothesis that has a set of disconnected tracks. For each hypothesis, the future position of the object in the next frame is predicted. Each of these predictions is compared using distance measures. MHT can track multiple objects and also handle occlusions.

Kernel-Based Tracking Methods

Kernel-based tracking methods measure a moving object's emerging region between frames. The object's movement can be a parametric motion such as a translation, conformal, affine, and so on. Technically, this refers to measuring the motion of the object using geometric shapes. The downside of using geometric shapes is the inability to differentiate the portions of the object or the backgrounds overlapping when the object is in motion. Some of the kernel-based tracking methods include simple template matching (this was first covered in Chapter 5, but we will revise the process summary here), meanshift method, support vector machine method (SVM), and layering-based tracking methods.

Simple Template Matching

Template matching is a method used to process digital images where a small part of an image that matches with an image template is identified iteratively in each frame. The matching process includes verifying the image portion with a template that has all the possible positions, and the success of the matching is measured by a numeric index that is calculated when compared.

Meanshift Method

The meanshift tracking method iteratively finds the area of a video frame that is most similar to the previously initialized model. This image region is stored as a histogram, and using the gradient method, the tracker is brought to a location that is more similar to the model. In object tracking algorithms, the target representation is mainly a rectangular or elliptical region. It contains the target model and target candidate. To characterize the target, a color histogram is chosen. The target model is generally represented by its probability density function (PDF). The target model is regularized by spatial masking with an asymmetric kernel. This is executed iteratively for each frame.

The following is the step-by-step implementation for the meanshift method for object tracking in a video. First you initialize the webcam and crop the region that has the object of interest. Then you plot a histogram for the current frame.

```
4   # Initialize webcam
5   cap = cv2.VideoCapture(0)
6
7   # take first frame of the video
8   ret, frame = cap.read()
9   print type(frame)
10
11  # setup default location of window
12  r, h, c, w = 240, 100, 400, 160
13  track_window = (c, r, w, h)
14
15  # Crop region of interest for tracking
16  roi = frame[r:r+h, c:c+w]
17
18  # Convert cropped window to HSV color space
```

```
19  hsv_roi =  cv2.cvtColor(roi, cv2.COLOR_BGR2HSV)
20
21  # Create a mask between the HSV bounds
22  lower_purple = np.array([125,0,0])
23  upper_purple = np.array([175,255,255])
24  mask = cv2.inRange(hsv_roi, lower_purple, upper_purple)
25
26  # Obtain the color histogram of the ROI
27  roi_hist = cv2.calcHist([hsv_roi], [0], mask, [180], [0,180])
28
29  # Normalize values to lie between the range 0, 255
30  cv2.normalize(roi_hist, roi_hist, 0, 255, cv2.NORM_MINMAX)
```

Define the termination criteria. The centroid shift computations should stop to make it finite, and the criteria either can be a fixed set of ten iterations or can be set to when the centroid is shifted by at least one pixel.

```
32  # Setup the termination criteria
33  # We stop calculating the centroid shift after ten
        iterations
34  # or if the centroid has moved at least 1 pixel
35  term_crit = ( cv2.TERM_CRITERIA_EPS | cv2.TERM_CRITERIA_
    COUNT, 10, 1 )
```

Iterate through each frame, calculate the histogram back projection, apply the meanshift method to get the new location and draw it on the window, and iterate until the condition terminates.

```
37  while True:
38
39      # Read webcam frame
40      ret, frame = cap.read()
41
```

```
42        if ret == True:

43

44            # Convert to HSV
45            hsv = cv2.cvtColor(frame, cv2.COLOR_BGR2HSV)

46

47            # Calculate the histogram back projection
48            # Each pixel's value is it's probability
49            dst = cv2.calcBackProject([hsv],[0],roi_hist,
              [0,180],1)

50

51            # apply meanshift to get the new location
52            ret, track_window = cv2.meanShift(dst, track_window,
              term_crit)

53

54            # Draw it on image
55            x, y, w, h = track_window
56            img2 = cv2.rectangle(frame, (x,y), (x+w, y+h), 255, 2)

57

58            cv2.imshow('Meansift Tracking', img2)

59

60            if cv2.waitKey(1) == 13: #13 is the Enter Key
61                break

62

63        else:
64            break
```

Figure 6-9 shows the output of the meanshift program.

Figure 6-9. *Output of the meanshift method*

Another variation of the meanshift method is the continuously adaptive meanshift (CAM) shift method. The meanshift method assumes a fixed-size window. CAM shift extends meanshift and applies meanshift iteratively until it converges. The window size per iteration is recomputed, and the orientation for the best fitting of the ellipse is also computed.

The following is the step-by-step implementation for the CAM shift method for object tracking in a video. First, initialize the webcam and crop the region that has the object of interest. Then, plot a histogram for the current frame.

```
4   # Initialize webcam
5   cap = cv2.VideoCapture(0)
6
7   # take first frame of the video
8   ret, frame = cap.read()
9
10  # setup default location of window
11  r, h, c, w = 240, 100, 400, 160
12  track_window = (c, r, w, h)
13
14  # Crop region of interest for tracking
15  roi = frame[r:r+h, c:c+w]
16
17  # Convert cropped window to HSV color space
18  hsv_roi =  cv2.cvtColor(roi, cv2.COLOR_BGR2HSV)
19
20  # Create a mask between the HSV bounds
21  lower_purple = np.array([130,60,60])
22  upper_purple = np.array([175,255,255])
23  mask = cv2.inRange(hsv_roi, lower_purple, upper_purple)
24
```

```
25  # Obtain the color histogram of the ROI
26  roi_hist = cv2.calcHist([hsv_roi], [0], mask, [180], [0,180])
27
28  # Normalize values to lie between the range 0, 255
29  cv2.normalize(roi_hist, roi_hist, 0, 255, cv2.NORM_MINMAX)
```

Define the termination criteria. The centroid shift computations should stop to make it finite, and the criteria either can be a fixed set of ten iterations or can be set to when the centroid is shifted by at least one pixel.

```
31  # Setup the termination criteria
32  # We stop calculating the centroid shift after ten iterations
33  # or if the centroid has moved at least 1 pixel
34  term_crit = ( cv2.TERM_CRITERIA_EPS | cv2.TERM_CRITERIA_
    COUNT, 10, 1 )
```

Iterate through each frame, calculate the histogram back projection, apply the CAM shift method to get the new location and draw it on the window, and iterate until the condition terminates. The difference between the meanshift method and the CAM shift method is that you use polylines to show the adaptive boxes that are computed by the CAM shift function.

```
36  while True:
37
38      # Read webcam frame
39      ret, frame = cap.read()
40
41      if ret == True:
42          # Convert to HSV
43          hsv = cv2.cvtColor(frame, cv2.COLOR_BGR2HSV)
44
```

```
45          # Calculate the histogram back projection
46          # Each pixel's value is it's probability
47          dst = cv2.calcBackProject([hsv],[0],roi_hist,[0,180],1)
48
49          # apply Camshift to get the new location
50          ret, track_window = cv2.CamShift(dst, track_window,
            term_crit)
51
52          # Draw it on image
53          # We use polylines to represent Adaptive box
54          pts = cv2.boxPoints(ret)
55          pts = np.int0(pts)
56          img2 = cv2.polylines(frame,[pts],True, 255,2)
57
58          cv2.imshow('Camshift Tracking', img2)
59
60          if cv2.waitKey(1) == 13: #13 is the Enter Key
61              break
62
63      else:
64          break
```

Figure 6-10 shows the output of the CAM shift program.

Figure 6-10. *Output of the CAM shift code*

The meanshift method will work well if there is prior knowledge of the object that needs to be tracked. The CAM shift method works well when the object that is being tracked changes shape with a changing camera perspective.

Support Vector Machine

The support vector machine (SVM) classification method provides both positive and negative training values to represent both sets of objects that are tracked and not tracked. This method can handle a single-image, partial occlusion of an object, but it is a prerequisite to initialize the model.

Layering-Based Tracking

Layering-based tracking uses kernel-based tracking to track multiple objects. Each layer consists of shape representation (ellipse), motion such as translation and rotation, and layer appearance based on intensity. Layering here is nothing but isolating the motion of the object that is tracked from the motion of the other parts or the background of the image. The probability of each pixel of the object being tracked is computed relative to the shape features and background motion.

Silhouette-Based Tracking

In most cases, objects don't have specific geometric contours, such as a human body, hand, fingers, and so on. Silhouette-based tracking does well tracking objects of this sort because it can support an accurate shape description for the objects. The objective of the silhouette-based object tracking method is to find the object in context from a region in every frame using the object model generated by the previous frames. This method supports flexible object shapes and object split and merge cases as well. This method has two approaches: contour tracking and shape matching.

Contour Tracking

Based on a primary contour defined in the initial frame, contour-based tracking iteratively uses the previously defined contour to its position in the current frame. This contour progress requires that a certain amount of the object in the current frame overlay the object region in the previous frame. Contour tracking can either use state space models to model the contour shape or use motion or gradient descent techniques.

Shape Matching

Shape matching is similar to the template-based tracking used in the kernel approach. Detection based on a silhouette is carried out by background subtraction. Model objects are in the form of density functions, silhouette boundaries, and object edges. It is capable of dealing with single objects and occlusion handling, which is performed with Hough transform techniques.

Conclusion

In this chapter, you learned how to track moving objects. The different steps involved in object tracking such as object detection, classification, and tracking were covered with approaches or methods for each step. For specific cases such as optical flow, techniques such as the Lucas–Kanade algorithm and dense optical flow algorithm were explained with step-by-step implementation guides. You also learned how to use the meanshift and CAM shift techniques to track moving objects in a video. You looked at what background subtraction is, why and where it is used, and how to implement the KNN approach in OpenCV 3.4.*x*.

This chapter concludes all the key OpenCV functions for implementing critical computer vision use cases.

Index

A

B

C

© Sunila Gollapudi 2019
S. Gollapudi, *Learn Computer Vision Using OpenCV*,
https://doi.org/10.1007/978-1-4842-4261-2

Printed in the United States
By Bookmasters